GW00391749

PROFIT SHARING
AND
PROFITABILITY

PROFIT SHARING
AND
PROFITABILITY

How Profit Sharing Promotes
Business Success

D Wallace Bell and
Charles G Hanson

Published in association
with the Institute of Personnel
Management

Kogan
Page

First published in Great Britain by
Kogan Page Limited 1987
120 Pentonville Road, London N1 9JN

Copyright © D. Wallace Bell and Charles G. Hanson 1987
All rights reserved

British Library Cataloguing in Publication Data
Bell, D. Wallace
    Profit sharing and profitability.
    1. Profit sharing 2. Profit
    I. Title   II. Hanson, Charles
    338.5'16   HD2971

    ISBN 1-85091-303-X

Printed and bound in Great Britain by
Billing & Son Ltd, Worcester

Contents

Acknowledgments

This book could not have been written without support and help from several people. We are especially grateful to:

The trustees of the Esmée Fairbairn Charitable Trust, for financial assistance.

Robert Watson, Lecturer in Accounting at the University of Newcastle, for an indispensable contribution to the comparison of profit sharing and non-profit sharing firms by taking the main responsibility for the computing aspects of that project. The computer facilities at the university were used during the project.

Helen Watson, for devotion to clerical duties in constructing a database for the comparison of profit sharing and non-profit sharing companies.

J. Remus, of FONDACT (France), for the section on profit sharing in France.

The Profit Sharing Research Foundation (USA), for providing material on which the section on profit sharing in the USA is based.

The Industrial Participation Association, for administrative support throughout the project.

Our publishers, for ensuring publication within six months of the book being completed.

The text has been carefully read and revised, but we accept full responsibility for any errors of fact or interpretation which remain.

D W B, C G H

Preface

The aim of this book

There has been more interest in profit sharing in Britain in the past few years than ever before, but no up-to-date and comprehensive book on the subject has been available. This book, which incorporates the results of extensive research into the economic performance of profit sharing companies as well as an examination of all the most important aspects of the topic, is intended to fill that gap.

In recent discussion there has been considerable confusion about the nature and purpose of profit sharing, so in Chapter 1 we try to clarify the issues. Profit sharing today is built on a legacy from the past, and in Chapter 2 we describe its development in the UK from the earliest schemes in the 19th century to the present. Chapter 3 examines employee attitudes in profit sharing companies, based on an attitude survey we undertook in 1984 with 2703 respondents in 12 companies.

Chapters 4 and 5 describe and report on our recent study comparing the economic performance of 113 profit sharing companies with that of 301 non-profit sharers over the period 1978–1985. The companies were all UK quoted companies, and their performance was measured by nine economic ratios for each of the eight years. The results reported in detail in Chapter 5 show that the profit sharing firms' performance was significantly better than that of the non-profit sharers, and Chapter 6 examines the reasons why. What are the characteristics that make profit sharing companies so successful?

Chapter 7 contains practical guidance for those who are considering the introduction of profit sharing into their own companies, whether public or private. In Chapters 8 and 9 we look first to the future of profit sharing in the UK, and then review its development in the three other countries where it is much more widespread than here: the USA, France and Japan.

The appendices provide more statistical data, by sector, about the comparative performance of profit sharing and non-profit sharing companies, and a list of the 113 profit sharing firms included in our research project.

The book is intended primarily for those who are directly concerned with the introduction or maintenance of profit sharing schemes, but also policymakers, investment managers, academics and all who are interested in the industrial, commercial and economic success of UK Limited.

CHAPTER 1

Profit sharing in the UK: its nature and purpose

The nature of profit sharing

Over the past several years there has been increasing interest in profit sharing, and more recently in proposals for profit-related pay. The two should not be confused. Profit sharing in the United Kingdom, and in all other countries in the Western world, has always been understood as providing an additional bonus, related to profit, over and above established wages or salaries. It is a sharing of profit between employers and employees, in a sense comparable to the dividends paid to the shareholders, and the rules of most profit sharing schemes specifically state that the scheme does not form any part of employees' contracts of employment, and that payments under it shall not constitute any part of their basic remuneration. Profit sharing bonuses may vary from year to year, or in some years may not be paid at all, but basic wage or salary rates are not thereby put at risk.

By contrast, in profit-related pay, part of the basic remuneration, possibly a substantial part, would be linked to profit, so that if profits fall, wages would fall in parallel. Profit sharing has been tested by long and wide experience in many countries; profit-related pay has been tried in only a few instances over a short period, mainly in atypical companies in the USA.

Profit sharing in the UK dates from the mid-nineteenth century, but, with some notable exceptions such as Imperial Chemical Industries, The Boots Company, and the John Lewis Partnership, until comparatively recently it was found mainly in medium size and smaller firms in manufacturing industry. From the mid-1970s, however, as we shall show in Chapter 2 on the history of profit sharing, it has spread rapidly among many leading companies, and is now more widespread, and on a more stable basis, than ever before. As a result largely of tax concessions introduced in the Finance Act 1978 for schemes in which the bonus is provided in the form of company shares, and concessions in the Finance Act 1980 for employee share option schemes, there has also been a renewal of employee share ownership which was a characteristic of many of the early profit sharing schemes in the nineteenth century.

Indeed, tax concessions apart, there is a close parallel between the position today and the philosophy reflected in the first issue of *Labour Co-partnership*, the journal of what was then the Labour Association and is now the Industrial Participation Association, in August 1894:

'By Co-partnership we understand that system under which, in the first place, a substantial and known share of the profit of a business belongs to the workers in it, not by right of any shares they may hold, or any other title, but simply by right of the labour they have contributed to make the profit; and in the second place, every worker is at liberty to invest his profit, or any other savings, in shares of the society, and so become a member entitled to vote on the affairs of the body which employs him'.

But concepts change, and accountancy becomes more sophisticated. Profit sharing today, as in the past, is still essentially a bonus, in some way related to profit, over and above the normal wage for the job, but it may or may not be described as profit sharing! Staff participation schemes, share participation, wealth sharing, gain sharing and prosperity sharing are other terms commonly used, while some schemes have copyright titles owned by the consultants who devised them. And the formulae by which the bonus is calculated also vary greatly. While many schemes are still based on a simple percentage of profit, others use return on capital employed, sales margin, the ratio of value added to payroll costs, or even the rate of dividend paid on the ordinary shares; and in a significant proportion of cases the bonus is discretionary and determined by the directors annually.

Even the concept that all employees (or all with a qualifying period of service) automatically participate in the scheme is no longer sacrosanct. In some schemes participation depends on the employees themselves making a contribution. The company offers to give one free share (or more than one) for every share purchased by the participant from his own resources – up to a given maximum. Is that profit sharing? Certainly not in the traditional sense, but in so far as the total sum made available by the company for distribution as free, or matching, shares is related to profit, it can be said to be profit sharing, but on a self-selection basis.

So today profit sharing is much more diverse than it used to be, and probably in the future it will become even more so. That is as it should be. If it were still set in a nineteenth century mould it would not fit many of our present industrial and commercial structures. But it is characteristic of profit sharing that whilst maintaining its essential elements, it can readily be adapted to varying circumstances and needs.

The purpose of profit sharing

Proponents of profit sharing are divided between those (mainly economists and politicians) who look to its potential long term impact at the macro level of the economy, and others (business managers) who, while they may subscribe to some of the macro objectives, are more concerned with the immediate impact at the micro level because it is they who have to decide whether or not to introduce profit sharing in their own firms.

At the macro level, it is suggested that widespread profit sharing, especially if associated with employee shareholding, could transform the climate of industrial relations because employees would see that their own interests were directly related to the success of the company and to the interests of its other shareholders. As a result, employees would join with management in striving to improve their firm's productivity and profitability, and this extended to companies generally would in turn stimulate the national economy. Some maintain that if profit sharing came to form a substantial part of total remuneration, the resulting pay flexibility would lead to a reduction in unemployment. And there are those who see employee shareholding as a step towards the wider social objective of a shareholding democracy.

The macro economists tend to project forward changes which they say would, or should, occur at the macro level if profit sharing were almost universally adopted at the micro level. They therefore advocate its adoption at this level in order to achieve their macro objectives. But reality is not like that. We know from the experience of more than 100 years of profit sharing that, although there have been similar arguments in the past, profit sharing has never become sufficiently widespread for it to have any significant impact at the macro level. That may begin to change if the rate of extension of profit sharing over the last ten years continues in the future, but it is unlikely to happen fast enough to satisfy the present objectives of its macro proponents. Nor would the effect on the economy of widespread profit sharing be entirely predictable. 'The economy' is not a precise model in which everything fits neatly together and a given stimulus will always lead to a predictable result. It is the sum of many different activities at any given time, and shaped by a variety of both internal and external pressures. We may believe that profit sharing must have a beneficial effect, and the more widespread it is the stronger that effect will be, but we cannot predict with certainty just what it will achieve.

For the present, however, and indeed for the foreseeable future, profit sharing will, and should, be introduced in individual firms for micro- rather than macro-economic reasons: because of managers' assessment of its appropriateness to their own companies and the effect they think it could have on them, not because of any contribution they feel it might make to the macro economy.

Pay and profit sharing

We should also keep things in perspective. The vast majority of employees are not involved in any form of financial participation except the two basic ones – wage or salary, and for an increasing number, a pension fund. And for about a third of the workforce – those in the public sector – that is, at present, the limit of what is practicable.

For all employees, however, whether in profit sharing firms or not, it is through the wage structure that they get, and will continue to get, the basic remuneration on which they depend for their livelihood. And the wage structure itself should be right before there is any consideration of profit sharing. There is no way of providing satisfaction through a profit sharing scheme if the wage structure is itself a source of discontent, and there is no way in which a profit sharing scheme can be used to put it right.

We share the concern of those who think that the present wage structure in much of British industry is far from satisfactory, and that the system of wage determination still operating in most large firms is never likely to get it right. Adversarial annual wage negotiations with employers generally trying to settle for something below the rate of inflation, and employees asking for, and usually getting, a fair bit above, without any relation to increased productivity, are calculated simply to perpetuate inflation and reduce competitiveness, and do not in the end satisfy anyone.

We also share the concern of those who want to see a closer relation between the economic performance of companies, whether measured by profit or some other factor, and pay. Profit sharing has always provided such a connection, because in any scheme with a fixed formula by which the profit sharing bonus is determined (and every scheme should have a fixed formula), when profits increase, the bonus increases, and when profits fall, the bonus falls – or it may disappear altogether. There is therefore flexibility of total remuneration, but without jeopardizing basic pay, the proper and adequate rate for the job.

That is very different from the proposals for profit-related pay that would link a substantial proportion of present wages to profit, and thus put employees' basic remuneration at risk if profits fall. In our view this is calculated to produce almost exactly the opposite effect from profit sharing.

Profit sharing has been seen by those who practise it as leading to a closer identification by employees with the companies for which they work. Profit-related pay would be unlikely to do so if employees felt that part of their established wage could be in jeopardy, possibly through management's mistakes.

Profit sharing gives employees a sense of security and satisfaction. They know that their basic pay is secure (short of disaster and losing their jobs), and they can look forward to something extra on top. Their eyes are on increasing profits and higher bonuses. A well-designed profit sharing scheme provides a positive encouragement to everyone to cooperate in constantly improving the company's performance, knowing that they will share in the rewards. But most employees more or less live up to their income, so with profit-related pay the knowledge that some of their basic pay is at risk could cause insecurity and anxiety. At all levels, including management, employees would be more likely to adopt a play-safe, defensive attitude in trying to maintain the current level of profit and so protect their pay, rather than making a positive drive to increase it.

It is notable that in an attitude survey among employees in 12 profit sharing companies which we undertook in 1984, 91% of the 2703 respondents were in favour of profit sharing, but 96% said it should not be a substitute for an adequate wage or salary.* We believe that is a fair reflection of employees' views generally, entirely justified, and not likely to change.

Management's objectives in profit sharing

In that survey and in other discussions we have also examined the motivation and objectives of the managements of companies that have introduced profit sharing. Two are almost invariably put first: to strengthen the sense of identity with the company, and to enable employees to share in its success. These have always been seen as the main reasons for, and objectives in, profit sharing, and they remain so today. And with share distribution schemes they are supplemented by a third: to enable employees to build up a personal stake in the company.

Many managements stop there; they feel that these objectives are sufficient in themselves, and if they can be achieved all the potential benefits of profit sharing will follow from them. Others are more specific, and many managers put as one of their main objectives, to encourage employees to take a greater interest in the company's profits and financial results. Indeed when management is increasingly encouraging employees to be concerned about their firm's profitability and performance, and providing them with more and more information through briefing groups, company newspapers, employee reports and so on, it does help to stimulate interest if employees know that they will be getting some of the profit that is being talked about. Otherwise, why should they care?

A further objective, less often stated openly but held by many managements, is to encourage employees to realise that by their own efforts they can contribute to the company's success and profitability. It is an objective that is not always achievable. Much depends on the nature of the company and the design of the profit sharing scheme. It would have little relevance in a large diversified multi-plant company with a scheme based on a small percentage of group profit, and even less if exchange rate or commodity price fluctuations could significantly affect that profit.

Less common objectives, or less commonly stated, are to strengthen participation, which presupposes that effective participation arrangements are already established, and competitive necessity – if employees can easily switch between different firms all offering much the same employment package but some have profit sharing on top, others may feel they need to introduce a scheme in order to

---

Profit Sharing and Employee Shareholding Attitude Survey, by D. Wallace Bell and Charles G. Hanson, Industrial Participation Association, 1984

attract and retain the calibre of employees they want. This was almost certainly a factor in the rapid spread of profit sharing in the 1970s among multiple retailers and High Street banks.

Some managers also see approved profit sharing schemes in which the bonus is provided in the form of company shares as providing a means of giving employees tax-efficient benefits, and some point to the favourable effect on the company's cash flow if new shares are issued for this purpose – these are perhaps accountants' motivations. And although it is not usually admitted, it is undoubtedly true that some managements are also influenced by fashion in deciding whether to introduce profit sharing: fashion in particular industries, or prevalent throughout industry.

There are two considerations which should not be among management objectives in any profit sharing scheme, and which would almost certainly guarantee its failure. The first is to pay lower wages than would otherwise be necessary. A company that follows this policy is not likely to attract the calibre of employees it will need for success, and its profitability may suffer in consequence. The second is to promote profit sharing as a direct incentive to individual employees to work harder in the hope of increasing their own bonus at the end of the year. Too many things outside the control of the employees can go wrong, and if profit sharing has been put across in this way, it will lead to disillusion and resentment when their expectations are not met.

At company level, therefore, what can be expected from profit sharing, as from other forms of employee involvement, is a stronger sense of identity with the company, and a greater willingness to cooperate with management in improving its performance. Most managers we have met in profit sharing companies have said that, at least to a modest extent, profit sharing, as part of their total employee participation arrangements, has had some effect in this direction. They felt that their objectives in introducing the scheme had by and large been met, and more significantly, they said that in the light of their experience of profit sharing, if a scheme did not already exist in their company they would certainly now introduce one.

That being so, why is profit sharing not much more widespread? The 700 or so profit sharing companies in the UK compares poorly with Japan, where profit sharing is a relatively recent innovation but is almost universal in mainstream companies; with the USA, where there are reportedly some 400 000 profit sharing firms; and with 12 000 in France.* In these countries, however, there have been special reasons for the spread of profit sharing which are not relevant to the UK. In Japan, profit sharing is the main source of personal savings against the five-year gap (previously ten years) between compulsory retirement in the larger companies and the qualifying age for pension. In the USA it is more common in small rather than

---

*A fuller description of profit sharing in these countries is given in Chapter 9

large firms, and was often introduced as a substitute for a pension scheme. And in France it is obligatory by law for all companies with more than 100 employees.

In the UK, however, there are no such external pressures for profit sharing, and its introduction depends entirely on the decision of the management of each individual company, and their assessment of its likely benefits. But 'decision' is perhaps the wrong word. In a research project commissioned by the Department of Employment in 1985 which explored the extent of profit sharing and employee share ownership schemes in the UK, it was found that of those companies that did not have any all-employee scheme (79% of the total surveyed) more than three-quarters (76%) had never even considered introducing one.*

More has been written and said about profit sharing in the last ten years than ever before, but despite this it seems so far to have failed to catch the attention or the imagination of most British managers. We hope that this book will do something to change that.

---

*Profit sharing and employee share ownership in Britain, by Gillian R. Smith, *Employment Gazette*, Sept. 1986

CHAPTER 2

The history and growth of profit sharing in the UK

The first recorded profit sharing scheme in the UK was started by Lord Wallscourt on his farms in Galway in 1829, but this was an isolated case and no further schemes came into existence until 1865. In that year six schemes were introduced, the best known being that in the coal mining company of Henry Briggs and Son. From 1865 onwards, although growth was erratic and intermittent, profit sharing continued to spread slowly until the rate of growth quickened perceptibly in the 1970s. In fact until the last ten or fifteen years the managing director who introduced profit sharing was often regarded as a benevolent but rather unconventional individualist.

Table 2.1 shows the increase in the number of schemes between 1829 and 1919.

Table 2.1 *Number of profit sharing schemes in the UK 1829–1919*

Year/ period	No. of schemes started	No. of schemes which had ceased to exist by 1919	No. of schemes still operating in 1919
1829	1	1	–
1865–69	17	15	2
1870–79	18	12	6
1880–89	49	38	11
1890–99	100	84	16
1900–09	79	32	47
1910–19	116	16	100
Total	380	198	182*

*Including six schemes described as suspended
Source: *Report on Profit Sharing and Labour Co-Partnership in the United Kingdom*, HMSO 1920, Cmnd 544, pp. 9–10.

In the early years enthusiasm for profit sharing went in waves which lasted for two, three or four years. The years 1889–92, 1908–09 and 1912–14 were periods of maximum activity, while 1893–1907 was a period of quiescence. In a very general way it seems that periods of enthusiasm for profit sharing coincided with periods when employment was good but, paradoxically, there was industrial unrest. Then, as often today, it may have been the unrest which prompted employers to consider new approaches in their employment policies.

Profit sharing was thinly spread among both farmers and manufacturers, but became particularly popular in the gas industry in the early twentieth century, with 37 gas companies introducing schemes between 1908 and 1914. For participants in schemes between 1901 and 1918 the average ratio of the profit sharing bonus to wages was 5.5%. In 1954 the comparable figure was 6.3%, so it seems that a typical payment has been the equivalent of about three weeks' wages.

It will be seen from Table 2.1 that by 1919 rather more schemes had ceased to exist than those which remained in existence. So it is hardly surprising that the comment was made in the 1920 Report that 'the most noticeable feature in the statistics of the Profit Sharing and Co-Partnership movement in this country as a whole is the large proportion of schemes which have ceased to exist'. And the further point was made that only 36 of the 182 schemes existing in 1919 had been started before 1901.

The reasons for failure were varied, but to some degree associated with the prevalence of profit sharing among relatively small firms. Some went out of business or were taken over. Others went through a period when there were no profits and the scheme just died. Sometimes the advent of trade union negotiations led to the bonus being consolidated into basic wage rates. In other cases profit sharing had been introduced in the expectation that it would act as an instant panacea for all industrial relations problems, and when the expectation was not fulfilled the scheme was discontinued. However, the fact that the number of schemes continued to grow indicates that the high casualty rate did not deter new enthusiasts from following the example of the early pioneers.

Table 2.2 shows the overall growth in profit sharing between 1894 and 1954. It is based on the official reports which were issued at fairly regular intervals during that period and immediately raises the question of why no comparable survey has been carried out since 1954.

Table 2.2 *The growth of profit sharing in the UK 1894–1954*

	1894	1912	1919	1938	1954
No. of companies	101	133	164	256	297
No. of employees	28 269	106 189	243 050	386 000	564 446
No. of participants	–	–	–	219 200	344 792

Sources: *Official Reports on Profit Sharing* 1894 (Cmnd 7458) 1912 (Cmnd 6496) and 1920 (Cmnd 544) and *Ministry of Labour Gazette* August 1939 and May 1956.

The figures show that despite the failure of many schemes, and the erratic and intermittent development of profit sharing, it continued to grow. To paraphrase the 1920 Report it might have been said that 'the most noticeable feature of profit sharing in Britain is its continuing growth despite many difficulties'. But this growth was slow, so that by 1954 the number of participants was still only 345 000, about 1.5% (or one in seventy) of the working population.

The Industrial Participation Association

In June 1884, a 'Committee for Promoting Cooperative Production' was established during the Annual Cooperative Congress in Derby. Subsequently this Committee became known as the Labour Association and in 1892 it presented a list of 80 profit sharing firms in its evidence to the Royal Commission on Labour, which was sitting at that time. In 1894 the Association's activities were supplemented by the publication of the journal *Labour Co-Partnership* and in 1902 the name was changed to 'Labour Co-Partnership Association' largely because profit sharing firms were becoming more numerous. Its objects were restated as 'To bring about an organization of industry based on the principles of Labour Co-Partnership; that is to say a system in which all those engaged shall share in the profit, capital, control and responsibility'. In 1927 the name was changed again to the 'Industrial Co-Partnership Association', but the programme of meetings and lectures and the publication of the journal continued as before. When the Association became known by its present title of Industrial Participation Association in 1972 its essential objective – to create a common purpose at work – was unchanged. And when the IPA celebrated its centenary in 1984 its corporate membership covered over three and a half million employees. Among other events the centenary year was marked by the publication of the extensive attitude survey among participants in profit sharing schemes which is summarized in the next chapter of this book.

The total income of the IPA in 1985 was only £126 000, but the influence of this Association has been out of all proportion to the modest scale of its operations. Its members, mainly business firms committed to a participative approach, have always seen profit sharing as a key element of that approach and many of them have introduced it. But clearly the best efforts of the IPA on its own will not be adequate to spread participation and profit sharing throughout the British economy. Nor has the repeated endorsement of employee participation in general and profit sharing in particular by successive Ministers of Labour and Secretaries of State for Employment made any great impact.

The Yellow Book of 1928

It is very rare for a mixed group of politicians, businessmen, trade unionists and academics to come together to formulate a long-term strategy for the British economy. But this is what happened in 1927 when leading Liberal politicians and some distinguished businessmen, trade unionists and economists who were broadly sympathetic to a Liberal point of view constructed a programme for 'Britain's Industrial Future', as they called it. Their substantial report, which was published in 1928, became widely known as *The Yellow Book*.

Perhaps the most important section of *The Yellow Book* was Book 3 'Industrial Relations', which was remarkably farsighted. One of the recommendations was 'definite legal protection' against unfair dismissal. It was 43 years before this was implemented in the Industrial Relations Act 1971, and it is now accepted as a normal part of our labour relations system. Other key sections in Book 3 were concerned with profit sharing, which the authors saw as an essential element in a sound system of remuneration for the worker. They were adamant that this element should be 'an addition to, and in no degree a substitution for' an employee's agreed standard wages. And they thought that it 'should consist of a share of residual profits after capital has received a fair return, proportionate to the risks it has to run'. This element, which they called profit sharing, was to be confined 'to cases in which employees receive, as contributors of labour and not of capital, a share of profits fixed in advance, and based upon their labour contribution'.

Having defined profit sharing, the authors went on to spell out its purposes in a crucial section, from which the following two paragraphs have been abstracted:

'The real purpose of profit sharing, in conjunction with the system of organised consultation which is described in the following chapters, is to show that the worker is treated as a partner and that the division of the proceeds of industry is not a mystery concealed from him, but is based upon known and established rules to which he is a party. If this end is to be secured, it is obviously essential (1) that the amount of the bonus should not depend upon the will of the employer, but should be determined by a scheme settled beforehand and clearly understood; and (2) that the workmen entitled to benefit under the scheme should be given access to such financial data as will show that it has been carried out. When this is done, the primary purpose of a true profit sharing scheme will be fulfilled even if there are no profits to divide…

'It is essential for the success of profit sharing that it should be generally realised that its primary object is not to bring about an increase of output per head, nor to increase directly the worker's remuneration (though both of these aims may be incidentally attained), but to improve industrial relations by making it clear that the product of industry is divided on known and established principles, and thus to facilitate cooperation in the pursuit of efficiency.' (pp. 199–200)

What kind of profit sharing scheme was to be preferred? And how was it to be encouraged? Both of these questions were answered in a way which is still relevant today:

> 'There can be no one "best" scheme of profit sharing; on the contrary, there ought to be a wide variation of method, according to the nature of the industry, the size and age of the business and the ratio between the amount of capital engaged and the number of employees'. (p. 202)

It was then pointed out that there were two main forms of profit sharing, with the bonus being distributed in cash or shares. The latter was to be preferred on the two grounds that it facilitated the creation of new capital and brought about a wider diffusion of ownership.

The view of the authors of *The Yellow Book* about profit sharing was summed up in their statement that it was 'of great importance that the system of profit sharing should be extended as widely and rapidly as possible'. But the Liberals were in the political wilderness and there was a time lag of exactly 50 years before positive steps were taken by government in 1978 to implement these recommendations.

The ICI profit sharing scheme 1954-1987

In 1987 the ambition of many of the brightest new graduates is to work in the City. In the 1950s and 1960s it was more likely to become a management trainee with Imperial Chemical Industries (ICI), a company which was a byword for efficiency and profitability. Right from the beginning top management at ICI have seen a participative management style as a key element in this efficiency and profitability.

The first chief executive, Sir Alfred Mond, who became Chairman and Joint Managing Director of the new enterprise when it was formed at the end of 1926, took personal responsibility for ICI's employment policies and presided at meetings of the Central Works Council. In two addresses to members of the Labour Co-Partnership Association earlier in 1926 he had insisted that the phrases 'employers and employed' and 'masters and men' were obsolete. 'The true phrase today is "co-workers in industry". They are co-workers in different capacities, and at different salaries, but are all dependent upon the prosperity of the industry for their remuneration or reward, whatever it may be'.* When he went on to examine 'practical methods of reform in the industrial organism' he gave co-partnership and profit sharing the highest priority: 'While not suggesting for one moment that there is any single avenue towards the establishment of an industrial Elysium, I am firmly convinced that cooperation in industry, particularly through co-partnership and profit sharing, is one of the most useful avenues by which the ultimate goal can be reached'.* ICI's experience is therefore a good illustration of the development of

---

*Sir Alfred Mond, *Industry and Politics*, Macmillan 1927, p. 110
*Ibid, p. 111

profit sharing, and the eventual introduction of a share-based scheme in 1954 underlines two vital truths. First, the effective implementation of participative employment policies requires the backing of the chief executive. And second, profit sharing is the culmination of a process, which in this case took 28 years.

The ICI scheme was by far the most extensive of its kind. The original number of participants was 81 000, rising to over 100 000 in the 1960s and 1970s and falling to approximately 53 500 in 1986 as the company was forced to slim its labour force in order to achieve the higher labour productivity necessary to compete successfully in new markets.

The ICI bonus is paid in the form of new ordinary stock of the company, issued for this purpose. Employees have always been free to sell their shares as soon as they receive them, and many do so. In 1978 the company introduced a new scheme under the provisions of the Finance Act 1978 to give employees the option of taking the whole or part of their bonus without income tax deduction, as deferred shares to be held by trustees for at least two years. This new scheme runs alongside the earlier scheme and the fact that in 1984 only 16% of employees chose the deferred shares with their substantial tax benefits indicates that the majority still want to be able to realize their bonus shares whenever they wish. Even so, the early introduction of share-based profit sharing meant that for many years ICI had a much higher proportion of employee shareholders than any other large British company.

The ICI scheme has always been relatively generous, with participants normally receiving a bonus of 5–10% of their earnings. In 1986 the total bonus payable (based on the 1985 results) was £49m with participants receiving an individual bonus of 8.1% on top of their earnings.

Like all good profit sharing schemes the ICI scheme is based on a predetermined and published formula. This was substantially changed in 1958, 1962 and 1964; and in 1978 the most significant change of all occurred when, following the recommendations of a joint working party, a new formula was introduced based on the relation between added value and employee costs. Further minor amendments were made in 1981 and it was agreed that the scheme should be reviewed at regular, five-yearly intervals. This shows that profit sharing, like every other aspect of a company's operations, requires constant monitoring and adjustment.

Commenting on an attitude survey among 214 participants in the scheme in 1984 the company stated that it was felt that

> 'the scheme has acted as an effective vehicle for promoting an understanding of the business, and of what needs to be done to remain competitive, and has led to an acceptance of change'.

It was also said that if ICI did not already have a profit sharing scheme, one would be introduced on the same basis as the existing scheme. Thus it was made clear that 30 years experience of profit sharing had not in any way diminished the commitment of the management of ICI to that particular form of employee participation. And the attitude survey mentioned above indicated that the commitment of employees to profit sharing was just as strong as that of management.

Two comments are appropriate to ICI's lengthy experience of share-based profit sharing. First, profit sharing may help the company to remain competitive, but it is no guarantee of commercial success. ICI was as badly hit by the recession of 1979–82 as many other manufacturing companies, and following a severe decline in profits no profit sharing bonus was paid in 1980 for the first and only occasion in the lifetime of the scheme. Perhaps this brought home to ICI employees more effectively than any other incident the need for the company to take drastic steps to improve its efficiency.

Second, ICI's satisfaction with profit sharing prompts the question 'Why did so few major companies follow ICI's example until the 1970s?' This is not an easy question to answer, especially when the 1960s was a decade of growing dissatisfaction with the state of labour relations in Britain. Perhaps the reluctance of most British managers to innovate in the field of profit sharing and employee shareholding during the period 1954–78 should be seen as evidence of a general malaise, among whose symptoms was an unwillingness to admit that the employment system needed a thorough overhaul. But from the mid 1970s onwards this attitude was shaken by the growing realization that the British economy was in serious relative decline and that poor labour relations were a contributory factor. At long last there was a willingness, albeit of a modest and cautious kind, on the part of businessmen and politicians to consider new approaches to employee relations including profit sharing.

The expansion of profit sharing 1974–1987

The number of firms in Britain practising profit sharing continued to grow, but despite the early enthusiasm of major firms like Vauxhall Motors (1935) and ICI (1954) growth remained erratic and slow. Then in the 1970s there was a quickening of interest in profit sharing so that by the end of that decade the movement included some of Britain's best known and most dynamic and profitable companies and was altogether more soundly based. It might be said that the period between 1974 and 1980 was the period when profit sharing in Britain finally came of age. Certainly in 1980 it was still a minority movement, but at long last the minority had to be taken seriously because of their success. The idea that profit sharing was often a short-lived fad was no longer credible in the face of the mass of contrary evidence.

The tax concessions for share-based profit sharing contained in the Finance Act 1978 were a substantial boost to this quickening of interest in profit sharing, but they were not the sole cause of it. From 1974 onwards a number of leading companies introduced schemes, including Wedgwood (china and pottery manufacturers, 1975) and the stores groups of Bentalls (1974) and Owen Owen (1974).

Even more significant was that all of the four major clearing banks in England had profit sharing by 1978.

The leaders were National Westminster and Barclays, who both introduced schemes in 1974. They were followed by Lloyds (1977) and the Midland (1978). This has wider significance for three reasons. First, every managing director has contact with one or more of the clearing banks and wants to convince them that his business is credit-worthy. Bank managers can hardly object to the introduction of profit sharing when they themselves are participating in a scheme. Second, the banks have always been regarded as somewhat conservative institutions in respect of labour relations. Therefore if profit sharing is acceptable to them, it should be acceptable to everyone else. Finally, the four major clearing banks are regarded as pillars of the financial and business establishment. Their viability is not open to question and there is, therefore, little or no possibility that their profit sharing schemes will fail.

For the major clearing banks to introduce profit sharing would have been unthinkable before the 1970s. It was a sure sign that the climate of opinion was changing. But the revolution (if it may be called that) was an almost silent one. How many people, even in 1987, are aware that profit sharing is almost complete throughout the banking sector in Britain and that the cashiers who serve them at their local branch may be shareholders in the bank for which they work?

Tax concessions in the Finance Acts 1978-85

The provision of tax concessions for approved profit sharing schemes in the Finance Act 1978 was a landmark in the history of profit sharing in Britain. It was another indication that the whole climate of opinion was beginning to change and gave a powerful boost to share-based profit sharing. The concessions were first introduced by a Labour government which needed Liberal support to maintain a majority in the House of Commons, but they had all-party backing, so that when a Conservative government was elected in 1979 there was no question of them being discontinued. In fact they were modified and extended between 1980 and 1985. The essence of the arrangement is that where the bonus is paid in the form of ordinary shares in the company for which the employee works, it is free of income tax provided the shares are held by trustees for a given period. The main conditions which have to be met before a scheme can be approved by the Inland Revenue are as follows:

1. The scheme must be open at least to all full-time UK employees of the company, including directors, who have completed a minimum period of service which may not exceed five years.
2. All such employees must be eligible to participate on similar terms.
3. The value of shares appropriated to any individual employee in any one year

may not exceed a stated maximum. (In 1978 this was £500. Now it is £1 250 or 10% of salary, whichever is greater, with a maximum of £5 000.)

4. The shares must be ordinary shares, fully paid up and non-redeemable, either in the company itself or in its parent company.

5. The shares must be held by trustees for a minimum period (the 'period of retention').

6. At any time after the period of retention an employee may require the trustees to sell the shares held on his behalf, or transfer them to his own name, but he will then be liable to pay income tax on their original value (or the sale proceeds if this is less) on a tapering scale dating from the time the shares were appropriated. This has been modified by successive Finance Acts and the position at present, compared with that in 1978, is as follows:

	1978 Finance Act	1985 Finance Act
No sale permitted	Years 1–5	Years 1–2
Income tax liability on:		
100% of value	Years 6–7	Years 3–4
75% of value	Year 8	Year 5
50% of value	Year 9	–
25% of value	Year 10	–
No income tax liability after	Year 10	Year 5

(In certain circumstances if an employee leaves the company involuntarily the shares may be sold during the retention period.)

7. While their shares are held by trustees, employees do not have the right to attend shareholders' meetings (although they may be invited to do so), but they have all the other rights of shareholders. They are entitled to dividends paid on the shares, they will receive all reports and accounts and other documents sent to shareholders, they may instruct the trustees how to vote on their behalf at shareholders' meetings, and the eventual decision whether to retain the shares or sell them is theirs alone, and the proceeds of the sale belong to them.

The money provided by the company to trustees to purchase scheme shares counts as a chargeable expense and is not subject to corporation tax. If the trustees then subscribe for newly issued shares, the money comes back into the company's cash flow. Thus share-based profit sharing, or co-partnership as it used to be called, has been made extremely attractive to companies and their employees. Not surprisingly, as Table 2.3 shows, several hundred firms have introduced approved schemes since 1978.

Table 2.3 *Submissions to and approvals by the Inland Revenue of all-employee share-based profit sharing schemes 1978–87*

Period	Submitted		Dropped	Approved	
	Annual total	Cumulative total	Cumulative total (estimate)	Annual total	Cumulative total
April 1978–March 1979	96	96		3	3
April 1979–March 1980	132	228		114	117
April 1980–March 1981	99	327		93	210
April 1981–March 1982	73	400		68	278
April 1982–March 1983	76	476	89	66	344
April 1983–March 1984	76	552	107	48	392
April 1984–March 1985	83	635	116	70	462
April 1985–March 1986	98	733	135	70	532
April 1986–March 1987	112	845	144	102	634

Source: Inland Revenue

Most new schemes introduced since 1978 have been approved by the Inland Revenue and most of the companies which already had profit sharing in 1978 have introduced an approved scheme to run alongside their previous scheme, which may have provided a cash bonus or shares which could be sold immediately. Thus some companies, such as ICI, now offer their employees a choice of taxed cash (or 'immediate' shares) or tax-free 'deferred' shares, while others simply offer deferred shares. It can be understood that many employees who were in the habit of receiving cash before 1978 have been reluctant to give up an immediately spendable bonus for deferred shares, but it seems that most of those who have never had the option of cash are well satisfied with deferred shares. In our 1984 Attitude Survey, 1207 of the respondents worked for companies which offered only deferred shares and 73% of this group stated that even if a (taxed) cash option were available they would still continue to take (untaxed) deferred shares. It seems to be the case that people do not miss what they have never had.

Extent of profit sharing in 1987

Between 1890 and 1954 regular surveys of the extent of profit sharing were carried out by the Labour Department of the Board of Trade and the Ministry of Labour. Indeed, articles including statistics on profit sharing were published in the *Labour Gazette* every year between 1895 and 1904. It might be imagined, therefore, that with the recent increased interest in the subject and the support of the tax concessions since 1978 there would today be more official information about profit sharing than ever before. Unfortunately the opposite is true and there are currently no reliable statistics, from government sources or elsewhere, of the number of firms with profit sharing schemes or of the number of participating employees. An attempt must therefore be made to produce 'guesstimates' although the reader should be aware that we make no claim as to their accuracy.

Tables 2.3 shows that 634 schemes had been approved by March 1987, but the Inland Revenue does not reveal the names of the companies involved. The reason given for this confidentiality is that some companies, after approval of their scheme, may decide not to introduce it and this could cause bad feeling among their employees. This may justify preserving confidentiality until an approved scheme has been introduced, but it is not a good reason for not publishing the names of those companies whose schemes have been approved and who have subsequently (probably within 12 months) introduced the scheme.

The most complete list of such companies of which we are aware is published by Extel Statistical Services. Their card for April 1987 listed 316 companies operating profit sharing schemes, but it was stated that the list 'does not purport to be entirely complete'. Although some of the 634 schemes approved by the Inland Revenue may not yet have been introduced, the majority would now be in operation. Thus we believe that there are at least 250 profit sharing companies omitted from the Extel list, and the figure may be as high as 300 or more. If these and all the smaller private profit sharing companies are taken into account, we believe that the total number of profit sharing companies at the time of writing (April 1987) is between 650 and 750.

The number of participants in schemes is even more difficult to estimate because we do not know the names of about half of the profit sharing firms. But the Extel list gives us a starting point. The number of employees of those 316 firms is about 2 176 000. As many as a third of them may not be eligible for profit sharing because they work outside the UK or have not completed the length-of-service qualification, so we may conclude that two-thirds, or about 1 451 000, participate in profit sharing. Then we have the difficult task of estimating the total number of employees of the other profit sharing firms. A few of these may be large, but on average they will probably be distinctly smaller than those on the Extel list. If we assume that there are at least another 400 profit sharing companies which have, on average, one-third of the number of employees and participants of those on the Extel list we must include another 918 000 employees and 612 000 participants. Thus in Table 2.4 we compare our 'guesstimate' of the extent of profit sharing in 1987 with the official figures for 1954:

Table 2.4 *The extent of profit sharing in the UK in 1954 and 1987*

	1954	1987
No. of companies	297	716
No. of employees	564 446	3 094 000
No. of participants	344 792	2 063 000

Sources: 1954 figures – *Ministry of Labour Gazette*, May 1956;
1987 figures – Estimates by the authors

We emphasize that we believe our figures err on the side of caution and we express the hope that a comprehensive official survey of the extent of profit sharing will soon be made. It would, in our view, also be useful for the Department of Employment, possibly in conjunction with the Industrial Participation Association, to maintain an up-to-date, voluntary register of profit sharing firms. This should include:

(a) name of profit sharing company,
(b) number of employees,
(c) number of profit sharing participants,
(d) total value of the most recent allocation.

There would be no compulsion for companies to register or provide details, but in our experience profit sharing companies are proud of their schemes and are usually willing to provide up-to-date information about them. It is most unlikely that they would refuse to provide the information mentioned above on an annual, voluntary basis. Once a register had been established, it would be a simple matter to keep it up-to-date.

What might be said about the increase in profit sharing between 1954 and 1987? Two comments are in order. First, the nearly six-fold increase in the number of participants is substantial; profit sharing is now far more extensive than it has ever been in the past. But (and it is a very big but) still only a relatively small number of companies have profit sharing schemes and only a small minority of UK employees participate in them.

A register of profit sharing firms, preferably published according to the sector of the economy in which the firms operate, would help to dispel the ignorance which currently surrounds the whole topic. It would show that profit sharing has spread more extensively in certain sectors as the firms in those sectors have taken steps to match their competitors. The banking sector has already been mentioned as one in which profit sharing is almost complete. The same is true of brewing where large (Bass) medium-sized (Vaux) and smaller (Burtonwood) breweries have adopted profit sharing over the past ten years. Many of the major multiple stores groups, including Burton, Storehouse, Marks and Spencer and Sainsbury also have schemes, but in most other sectors of the economy progress has been relatively slow. This is in contrast to earlier periods when profit sharing was more concentrated in smaller manufacturing firms which were often family businesses. If today's professional managers in these sectors came to realize that profit sharing could help to generate the involvement of all employees in the affairs of the company and their commitment to its success, this might do something to restore the manufacturing base of British industry.

CHAPTER 3

Employee attitudes in profit sharing companies

By 1983 profit sharing was spreading quite rapidly and claims were being made in several places, including the House of Commons, that it helped to improve the attitudes of employees towards their companies. But there was no hard evidence to support this claim. The best evidence, which can only be obtained from the participating employees themselves, requires an extensive survey of a random sample of employees in profit sharing firms responding to a carefully prepared confidential questionnaire. Such a survey is difficult to conduct, because it is never easy to win the support of management for what is inevitably a time-consuming operation, or to get an adequate number of replies from manual employees. However, in 1983 we decided that the time was ripe to carry out a survey of this kind and financial support from the Wincott Foundation together with support in kind from the Industrial Participation Association (of which Wallace Bell was Director at the time) enabled us to go ahead.

The five fundamental questions which we tried to answer were:

1. How favourably do participants react to profit sharing?
2. Does it change their perception of the firm and, if so, how?
3. Does it stimulate their interest in the firm's financial performance and profitability?
4. Do participants understand their scheme?
5. Do they prefer cash or shares as a bonus?

All the forty or so questions we asked were related directly or indirectly to one of these issues.

The survey was carried out by means of a two-part questionnaire which took about half an hour to complete. Part 1, which was common to all companies, contained more general questions about profit sharing and the attitudes of employees towards it. Part 2 was more particular and varied according to the nature of the schemes:

(a) those operating entirely under the provisions of the 1978 Finance Act, in which all the participants received their bonus tax-free in the form of ordinary shares in the company;

(b) those in which participants had the choice of taking all or part of their bonus in tax-free shares or taxed cash;

(c) those few schemes where the choice was between tax-free shares or unrestricted but taxed shares.

Questionnaires were distributed to a random sample of 4 060 employees in 12 profit sharing companies late in 1983 and early in 1984, and 2 703 were returned (a response rate of 67%). The confidentiality of the survey was emphasized and in most cases sealed envelopes containing the completed questionnaires were returned initially to the company's personnel department and then sent, unopened, to the University of Newcastle upon Tyne for checking and processing through the university computer.

Analysis of response

The questionnaire consisted mainly of questions with two to six possible discrete answers. These questions and the optional answers were labelled and punched onto the file in batches, with each batch consisting of all the completed questionnaires for one company. Only positive answers were used in the analysis; that is to say the percentage figures for each response refer only to those who answered that particular question.

On completion of all batches the 12 files were combined and the full sample was dealt with as follows:

(a) All Part 1s – a total of 2 703 cases – were analysed.

(b) The Part 2s were grouped into the three separate categories: deferred shares only, cash or deferred shares, and immediate or deferred shares. Each of the three groups was then analysed separately.

In addition, the analysis for each participating company was sent to the management of that company as soon as it was ready, and an appointment made with the relevant executives to discuss their view of the profit sharing scheme in the light of the survey results.

The tables 3.1 and 3.2 give comprehensive details of the sample of respondents by type of scheme and employee characteristics. Table 3.1 lists the 12 companies by name and categorizes them and the number of respondents by the type of scheme. Table 3.2 describes the respondents by length of service, age, job grade, sex and trade union membership. The tables taken together show that the sample was broadly based and generally typical of employees in the private sector, although there were relatively few participants from smaller companies (less than 500 employees).

Table 3.1 *Type of profit sharing scheme*

Participating companies	Number of respondents	
Schemes providing deferred shares only		
1. British Home Stores PLC	268	
2. H.P. Bulmer Holdings PLC	204	
3. The Burton Group PLC	218	
4. Provincial Insurance PLC	253	
5. W.H. Smith & Son (Holdings) PLC	198	
6. Whatman Reeve Angel PLC	66	
		1 207
Schemes providing option between cash and deferred shares		
7. Barclays Bank PLC	200	
8. The Boots Company PLC	453	
9. Richard Clay PLC	130	
10. Midland Bank PLC	202	
		985
Schemes providing option between immediate and deferred shares		
11. Imperial Chemical Industries PLC	214	
12. Marks and Spencer PLC	297	511
Total		2 703

Table 3.2 *Characteristics of respondents*

Length of Service	%	Job Grade	%
Under 2 years	1	Clerical/General	59
2–5	16	Supervisory	27
5–10	34	Managerial	14
10–20	30	Total	100
Over 20	19		
Total	100	Sex	%
		Male	47
		Female	53
		Total	100

Age	%	Membership of Trade Union or Staff Association	%
Under 21 years	5		
21–29	24		
30–39	22		
40–49	21	Members	56
50 and above	28	Non-Members	44
Total	100	Total	100

There are four sets of results to be considered:

- the composite results of the 2 703 responses to Part 1 of the questionnaire;
- the composite results to Part 2, being the responses from participants in the three different types of profit sharing scheme as set out in Table 3.1;
- the separate responses from participants in the 12 companies;
- the reaction of management to the results.

All of these four sets of results will be considered in the summary which follows, but most emphasis will be placed on the 2 703 responses to Part 1.

The composite results: analysis of the responses to Part 1

The first two questions set the tone of the survey and the response to them was as shown in Table 3.3.

Table 3.3

	%
1. How do you view profit sharing in general?	
It is an excellent idea	70
There is something to be said for it	21
I have no strong feelings for or against it	9
I am opposed to profit sharing	–
2. How do you view the profit sharing scheme in your firm?	
I am very much in favour of it	64
I favour the scheme, but I have reservations about matters of detail	24
I have no strong feelings for or against it	12
I am opposed to the scheme and would like it to be terminated	–

It is clear from these responses that there is strong support both for profit sharing in general (91%) and for particular profit sharing schemes (88%) from those who have experienced it. Support was only slightly stronger among managerial grades than among those we graded as clerical/general (e.g. shop assistants, warehousemen or bank clerks) and union members were slightly more enthusiastic than non-members. Was there no opposition whatsoever? A complete absence of opposition would be strange when for some (but seemingly a very few) 'profit' is one of the dirtiest words in the English language. In fact seven respondents expressed opposition to profit sharing and 12 wanted their companies' schemes to be terminated. However, as our results were all rounded to the nearest percentage point, this very low level of opposition was not reflected in the published report.

Then a number of questions asked respondents what they thought about the effect of profit sharing on employee attitudes generally. Results are given in Table 3.4.

Table 3.4 *Responses to the request: 'Please indicate your reaction to the following nine statements, ticking one box in each case'*

	Agree Strongly (%)	Agree (%)	Don't Know (%)	Disagree (%)	Disagree Strongly (%)
1. Profit sharing creates a better atmosphere in the firm	10	55	16	18	1
2. It is popular because people like to have the bonus	24	69	4	3	–
3. It makes people take a greater interest in profits and financial results	11	65	7	16	1
4. It is good for the company and the employees	14	72	11	3	–
5. It strengthens people's loyalty to the firm	6	41	17	34	2
6. It makes people try to work more effectively so as to help the firm to be successful	6	45	15	31	3
7. It is welcomed by the participants but should not be seen as a substitute for an adequate wage or salary	44	52	3	1	–
8. Most people are apathetic about profit sharing	2	22	25	47	4
9. It can cause disappointment or bitterness, because profits can go down as well as up	3	39	10	45	3

Taking the first two columns together ('agree strongly' and 'agree') it might be thought that the most significant responses are to statement 1 (creates a better atmosphere: 65%); statement 3 (greater interest in profits and financial results: 76%); and statement 6 (trying to help the firm to be more successful: 51%). It is not surprising, but it is nevertheless very significant, that 96% think that profit sharing 'should not be seen as a substitute for an adequate wage or salary'. This response from such a large sample of profit sharing participants is solid vindication of the views of those who have always argued that profit sharing should be an addition to, and never a substitute for, a normal wage. The response to statement 9 indicates that whereas 42% agree that profit sharing 'can cause disappointment or bitterness because profits can go down as well as up', 48% disagree with that statement. It would seem, therefore, that a significant proportion are prepared to accept with equanimity a reduction in, or even perhaps the elimination of, the bonus in hard times.

Then there followed what might be regarded as the two most important questions in the survey. They were both concerned with the way in which profit sharing changes employee attitudes. The first (Table 3.5) could only be answered by those respondents (1890 or 70%) who had previously worked for a non-profit sharing firm or had been with their present firm before profit sharing started.

Table 3.5 *Response to the question: 'In your experience does the existence of profit sharing improve employee attitudes in a company?'*

	%
Yes, it leads to a significant improvement	14
Yes, to a modest extent	59
No, it makes no difference	27
No, it makes them worse	–

Thus a large majority, 73%, thought that profit sharing did improve employee attitudes in a company. But did it change their own view of the company? The question was put immediately afterwards (Table 3.6) to all who had been with their present employer before profit sharing was introduced.

Table 3.6 *Response to the question: 'Thinking back to the introduction of profit sharing how did it change your view of the company as an employer?'*

	%
Very significantly for the better	23
Moderately for the better	45
Not to any significant extent	31
If anything, for the worse	1 (10)

Still a large majority (68%) stated that the introduction of profit sharing had improved their own view of their company as an employer. Taking the answers to these two questions together, it is reasonable to conclude that profit sharing does improve employee attitudes and employees' views of their company.

Finally, two questions were asked about the participants' understanding of their schemes. These revealed that 57% felt that they had a good knowledge of how the scheme worked, but 40% were unaware of, had not read or could not understand the literature about it provided by their company (in one firm the figure was 70%). This was a matter of concern to several of the companies in the survey. It is sometimes overlooked that the existence of a profit sharing scheme requires an ongoing programme of education among all participants, whose understanding of their scheme can never be taken for granted.

The composite results to Part 2

Responses from 1 207 participants in six companies who received deferred shares only*

The first – and perhaps the most important – question was a general one asking participants how far the acquisition of shares through the profit sharing scheme had altered their perception of the company. The effect had been positive for 57% of participants, with 9% stating that their perception of the company had been altered 'very considerably' and 48% 'to a modest extent'. By contrast 42% thought that 'it had not altered their perception of the company in any noticeable way' and 1% had 'if anything, a worse view of the company as a result of the scheme'. Perhaps the fairest conclusion from this varied response is that a share-based bonus on its own is not enough for many employees. In fact the spread of positive responses among these six companies was 48–67%. As the answers to the questions about participants' understanding of their schemes also indicated, some companies have been more successful than others in ensuring that employees understand profit sharing.

Another question asked employees how much interest they took in their shares. In response 68% said that they 'watched the share price from time to time to see how it is moving'. And to a further question which applied only to those who had held shares for more than two years, and asked how long they intended to retain them, 85% replied that they 'intended to hold their shares more or less permanently'.

Thus it seems that a large majority of employee shareholders take a long-term view of their shareholding and intend to keep their shares well beyond the end of the compulsory two-year holding period. At the same time more than two-thirds like to keep an eye on the value of their shareholding. Both of these attitudes are surely healthy ones.

But if employees watch the share price they will be aware that it fluctuates. When asked how they would react to a falling share price, 55% replied that they 'would not be concerned' by such a situation; another 41% 'would be concerned, but would have to accept the situation'; and only 4% 'would be very concerned and would feel that they were being robbed of a part of their profit sharing bonus'. This response suggests a quite sophisticated attitude towards the vagaries of the stock market.

Finally, these employee shareholders were asked whether they would have preferred a cash bonus, firstly in the absence of tax concessions for deferred shares, and secondly, given the existence of those concessions: 48% said they would choose shares even without any tax benefit; rising to 73% with the tax concessions. Taken together the answers to these questions suggest that a high proportion of those who

---

*At the time of the survey (1983–84) these shares were held by trustees for at least two years and only became completely free of income tax after seven years

have experienced being a shareholder in the company for which they work want to maintain that position and increase their holding; and that the tax relief provisions of the Finance Acts significantly increase that proportion.

Responses from 985 participants in four companies who may take cash or deferred shares

The most important question for these participants was a simple one: 'Did you take your most recent bonus in cash or shares?' Cash was chosen by 80%, shares by 20%.

At first sight the answer to this question might seem to contradict the previous answers in which a high proportion said they preferred shares. But in fact there is no direct comparison. The employees in the four companies in this latter group had all been used to receiving cash bonuses – in two companies for many years. Thus most had probably come to count on the bonus to help meet some regular annual expense such as holidays. The share schemes were subsequently introduced to give them the opportunity to take (untaxed) shares rather than (taxed) cash. Not surprisingly a majority were unwilling to forego the immediate advantages of a cash bonus.

Further questions were asked of those who had chosen cash and those who had chosen shares. Readers who wish to explore the detail of these answers should refer to the full report.

Responses from 511 participants in two companies who may take immediate or deferred shares

Once again much the most important question for these participants was the first: 'Did you take your most recent allocation in immediate (unrestricted) or deferred shares?' Immediate shares were chosen by 47%; deferred shares by 53%.

The figures seem straightforward, but this may be a classic case of aggregate statistics concealing more than they reveal. The two companies to which these figures refer are ICI and Marks and Spencer and for historical reasons there was a major discrepancy between them. Breaking the figures down, the response was as follows:

ICI (214 respondents)
Immediate shares: 84%
Deferred shares: 16%

Marks and Spencer (297 respondents)
Immediate shares: 21%
Deferred shares: 79%

As mentioned in Chapter 2, ICI started an immediate share scheme in 1954, long before tax concessions for profit sharing were thought about. Consequently, all ICI employees were used to the idea of receiving a bonus which could be converted into cash quite quickly, and when a deferred share scheme was introduced in 1978 it is not surprising that most preferred to continue to receive the immediate shares with no restriction on when they could be sold. But the Marks and Spencer immediate share scheme had only been operating for one year when a Finance Act scheme was introduced alongside it in 1979.

The combined figures for the two companies must, therefore, be treated with caution.

The separate responses from participants in the 12 companies

All that will be said here is that the composite responses obviously conceal differences between the responses from participants in separate companies. The clearest example of this is between the respondents in ICI and Marks and Spencer in their choice of immediate or deferred shares. There are always reasons for differences of this kind, but they are not always immediately obvious. They will usually be found in the different ways in which profit sharing has developed and employment conditions differ from one company to another. Each company has a certain culture of its own which influences the way in which its employees react. Those readers who are particularly interested in the detailed differences should refer to the original report, where the responses are set out company by company.

Management's reaction to the results of the survey

Our discussions with management in each of the 12 participating companies, after they had seen the analysis of the results for their firm, were an important part of the survey. How would management react to a candid view of its profit sharing scheme by a random sample of employees?

The summary of the results set out in this chapter indicates that participants generally were well satisfied, not to say enthusiastic, about the whole idea. It would have been surprising if this satisfaction were not reflected in management's view of the survey results. In each of the 12 companies management unhesitatingly reaffirmed its commitment to profit sharing and stated that in its view most of the scheme's objectives were being met. In five companies management said that if profit sharing did not exist, a scheme identical to the present one would be introduced. In the other seven companies the commitment to profit sharing was equally strong, but it was felt that modest amendments to the existing scheme might be needed or that more effort should be made to ensure that participants became more familiar with its workings. The general reaction of management, however, could be summed up as: 'The survey confirms our view that profit sharing is good for our company and we fully intend to maintain our commitment to it'.

Taking this view along with the findings of Chapter 2, it is surely fair to conclude that for many leading British companies profit sharing is now seen as an important and permanent part of their management philosophy. And in the light of our 1984 attitude survey results management can be confident that this policy is well supported by a large majority of their employees.

CHAPTER 4

Profit sharing and profitability: the background to the project

When our attitude survey was published in November 1984 we were asked by several people, including financial analysts, whether our research had produced any evidence that profit sharing companies were more profitable than non-profit sharers. It was not surprising that employees liked profit sharing, they said, but was profit sharing good for the company?

It had not been our intention to examine this question in the attitude survey, and the nature of the survey was such that even if it had been, any conclusions would have been unreliable. We had questioned a large cross-section of employees in 12 profit sharing companies, and while the number of employees was quite sufficient for statistical reliability, the number of companies was not, and we had made no comparisons with non-profit sharing firms.

It was, however, a legitimate question. Some research in the USA had shown a direct correlation between profit sharing and profitability, but the findings were based on a small number of companies, not representative of American industry as a whole. Some advocates of profit sharing in the UK had also claimed that profit sharing leads to improved performance, but there was no hard evidence to support their view. A large-scale survey based on a substantial number of both profit sharing and non-profit sharing companies, using a range of economic ratios and covering several years, was clearly necessary for any legitimate conclusions to be drawn. It should also compare like with like: engineering firms with other engineers, stores with stores and so on.

We therefore prepared an outline project that would be based on companies having a full quotation on the London Stock Exchange over the whole period

1976–1985, broken down into the different sectors listed in the *Financial Times*, and using nine different economic ratios measuring profitability, growth and investor returns. We excluded sectors that were not reasonably homogeneous (e.g. leisure) or where the number of companies that met our criteria were too few (e.g. hotels and caterers), also finance companies and natural resources. This left us with 827 companies in ten sectors:

beers, wines and spirits
building, timber, roads
chemicals, plastics
drapery and stores
electricals
engineering
food, groceries, etc
industrials (miscellaneous)
paper, printing, advertising
textiles.

We had decided to base the survey on companies with a full stock market quotation because the essential data we needed for them was available from published sources. It would have been unrealistic to assume that a sufficient number of companies would have been willing to provide all the detailed information we required, covering several financial years. But we also needed to know for each company whether or not it operated a profit sharing scheme, and if so, when it had started. This information was not available on a sufficiently reliable basis from independent sources, so in October 1985 a personally addressed letter was sent from the Industrial Participation Association to the company secretaries of all 827 companies, asking for their cooperation (Figure 4.1). It was accompanied by a reply card (Figure 4.2) and a stamped addressed reply envelope. We also asked whether, if the company did have a profit sharing scheme, it was an approved scheme under the provisions of the Finance Act 1978, and we invited additional comments.

Replies were received from 470 companies (a 56.8% response) but 11 replies were useless for our purpose because they did not give the name of the company. Of the 459 valid replies, 149 said they had profit sharing; 310 said they did not. Nine of the non-profit sharers were eventually eliminated from the project because on further examination we found they were subsidiaries of foreign companies, or their operations were almost entirely overseas. This left 301 non-profit sharing companies which have been included in the project.

There were a few companies that had not replied but were known to us to have long-established profit sharing schemes, and these were included after confirmation by telephone. This brought the total number of profit sharers to 157, of which 125 had schemes approved under the provisions of the Finance Act 1978. Several of

INDUSTRIAL PARTICIPATION ASSOCIATION

18 October 1985

85 TOOLEY STREET LONDON SE1 2QZ   Telephone 01-403 6018

J Smith Esq
Company Secretary
XYZ Company PLC

Dear *Mr Smith*

With the increasing interest in profit sharing and employee
shareholding, we are undertaking a survey of the economic
performance of profit sharing companies compared with other firms
in their sector. To do this we need to identify which companies do
have profit sharing schemes, and how long they have been in
operation. The purpose of this letter is therefore to ask if you
will be kind enough to help us by providing this information on the
enclosed card.

If your firm does not have profit sharing, all you need do is fill
in the company's name and tick the 'NO' box. But if you do have
profit sharing, the information on the card is all we shall need to
ask from you, as the survey will be limited to companies quoted on
the London Stock Exchange for which all other information needed is
available elsewhere. For your convenience, a stamped addressed
reply envelope is also enclosed.

In the survey report, individual company performance will not be
identified against company names - names will be given, if at all,
only in a list of firms that do have profit sharing.

I am sure you will appreciate that it is especially important to us
that you should respond to this request if your company does have a
profit sharing scheme.

With many thanks.

Sincerely

D Wallace Bell

PRESIDENT:
LORD VINSON OF RODDAM DENE LVO
CHAIRMAN: SIR RICHARD O'BRIEN
DEPUTY PRESIDENT:
F. J. MOORFOOT CBE
DEPUTY CHAIRMAN:
SIR JOHN BOYD CBE FRSA OF
DIRECTOR: D. WALLACE BELL OBE

Company limited by Guarantee
Registered in England No. 648436
Registered office as above

FOUNDED 1884: TOWARDS A COMMON PURPOSE AT WORK

Figure 4.1   *Letter sent to 827 companies*

INDUSTRIAL PARTICIPATION ASSOCIATION
85 Tooley Street, London SE1 2QZ
Tel: 01-403 6018

Name of company ....

	Yes	No
Does the company have a profit sharing scheme	☐	☐

If 'YES'

In what year did it start? ....

	Yes	No
Is the scheme approved under the provisions of Finance Act 1978?	☐	☐

Any comments you may wish to add ....

....

Figure 4.2 *The reply card*

these profit sharing companies, however, had introduced schemes only in the last few years. For the purpose of our project, should they be regarded as profit sharers or non-profit sharers?

We had determined that the project should examine companies' performance over eight of their financial years, 1977/78 to 1984/85, with 1976/77 as the base year for comparison in respect of growth factors and investor returns. We decided to include as profit sharers only those companies that had introduced schemes by 1980/81 or earlier, so that they actually had schemes in operation for at least four of the eight years covered by the project. In coming to this decision we had in mind that profit sharing schemes, especially approved schemes which most of the more recent ones are, usually take a year or more to prepare, and often have been under consideration for much longer. Profit sharing may therefore have been 'in the air', and beginning to influence attitudes in these companies well before the schemes were actually introduced. But for companies with schemes starting only in 1980/81 we decided also to make 'before and after' comparisons of their performance in the first four years covered by our project, and the last four.

Companies which had introduced profit sharing only in the last four years, from 1981/82 to 1984/85, we have not counted either as profit sharers or as non-profit sharers. They have been eliminated from the project altogether. There were 44 such companies.

We were therefore left with 113 profit sharing companies. Table 4.1 shows the distribution of these companies by the year in which profit sharing was introduced.

We then found that in three of our original ten sectors we were left with too small a number of either profit sharers or non-profit sharers for valid comparisons to be made. These were beers, wines and spirits; paper, printing, advertising; and textiles. The companies in these sectors have therefore been included with those in the *Financial Times* classification 'Industrials (miscellaneous)' to form the group we describe simply as 'miscellaneous'. The resultant seven sectors each have what we decided should be the minimum of six companies in each category. Table 4.2 shows the distribution of both profit sharing and non-profit sharing companies in them.

Table 4.1 *Distribution of profit sharing companies by year in which profit sharing introduced*

Year/ period	No. of companies	%
Before 1977	34	30.1
1977/78	2	1.8
1978/79	5	4.4
1979/80	24	21.2
1980/81	48	42.5
Total	113	100.0

Table 4.2 *Distribution of profit sharing and non-profit sharing companies by sector*

Sector	No. of profit sharing companies	No. of non-profit sharing companies	Total
Building, timber, roads	10	40	50
Chemicals, plastics	6	12	18
Drapery and stores	19	25	44
Electricals	6	23	29
Engineering	10	59	69
Food, groceries, etc	8	21	29
Miscellaneous*	54	121	175
Totals	113	301	414

*Includes beers, wines and spirits; industrials (miscellaneous); paper, printing, advertising; textiles.

From the point of view of our project, the only difference between the two groups of companies (profit sharing and non-profit sharing) is that the companies in one group all had profit sharing schemes in operation not later than 1980/81, whereas none of the companies in the other group had such schemes at least until after the end of their financial year 1984/85.

For each of the 414 companies (113 profit sharers, 301 non-profit sharers) the following information was compiled, for each of the years 1976/77 to 1984/85:

shareholders' funds
capital employed
turnover
pre-tax profit
earnings per share
dividends per share.

To this was added the industrial sector in which the company was placed, the date when its financial year ends, and in the case of profit sharing companies, the year profit sharing started. Except for the date when profit sharing started, which was taken from the replies received by the Industrial Participation Association, the main source of information was The Hambro Company Guide (October 1981 to November 1986) supplemented when necessary from Extel Cards.

All this information was fed into the Newcastle upon Tyne University computer, and from another computer tape (the London Share Price Data Tape) the annualized percentage total return to investors was included for each company for each of the years 1978 to 1985 inclusive. In all there were more than 29 000 separate pieces of information.

It is on this data, and the computer analyses derived from it, that our findings are based. The comparisons betwen profit sharing and non-profit sharing companies have been made for all companies combined, and also on a sector by sector basis. The composite results, which will be of most interest to the general reader, are reported and examined in detail in Chapter 5. Sector results, which will probably be of more interest to other companies in the same sectors, are in Appendix 1. Lists of the profit sharing companies in each sector are given in Appendix 2.

CHAPTER 5

Profit sharing and non-profit sharing companies compared

The aim of our project was to compare the economic performance of profit sharing companies with that of non-profit sharers. Was it better, worse, or much the same? The basis of comparison was therefore the performance of the non-profit sharing companies, against which we measured the record of the profit sharers.

We were not, however, comparing the performance of any one profit sharing firm with that of any one non-profit sharer. We have taken the performance of the 113 profit sharing companies as a group, and that of the 301 non-profit sharers as a group, and compared the performance of these two groups; and similarly, but with smaller numbers, in the sector comparisons. So as to do this without distortions arising from, for example, variations in the size of companies, ratios have been used to convert the raw data from each company into comparable measures, in most cases expressed as a percentage. Without this the multi-million pound profit of one very large company could not realistically be compared with the one million of a much smaller firm, and if the actual profit figures were used without adjustment, results of the larger companies would dwarf those of smaller ones. If, however, for each company its profit is shown as a percentage of shareholders' funds, or of capital employed, or of sales, size becomes irrelevant and large can legitimately be compared with small.

This is what we have done. To illustrate from return on shareholders' funds, the percentage ratio for each company has been calculated separately for each year, and then the percentages for all the profit sharing companies have been added together and divided by the number of companies to give the mean average; and similarly for the non-profit sharers. Thus we have the average performance of all the profit sharers which we can then compare with the average of all the non-profit sharers. And in arriving at the average, the performance of each company is given equal weight.

A further advantage of this method is that it has enabled us to take losses as well as profits into account. For some companies in some years profit ratios were negative, and these negative results are reflected in the averages. It also meant that in the few cases where full data was not available for a particular company for any one year, its relevant ratio could be omitted for that year without significantly affecting the average.

The ratios we have used to compare performance relate to:

1. Profitability:
   (a) Return on equity
   (b) Return on capital employed
   (c) Earnings per share
   (d) Return on sales

2. Growth:
   (a) Growth in sales
   (b) Growth in equity
   (c) Growth in profit

3. Investor returns:
   (a) Dividends per share
   (b) Total annual returns

(The meaning of these terms is explained under each heading in the pages that follow.)

The eight years 1977/78 to 1984/85 for which comparisons are made represent for each company its financial year ending on or before 31 December in the latter year, i.e. the data for a company's financial year ending at any time during 1978 is included in the year 1977/78. The only exception is total annual investor returns, which are based on calendar years beginning with 1978.

Profitability ratios

Return on equity

Return on equity is one of the most significant of all economic indicators. It shows the percentage return of pre-tax profit on shareholders' funds, i.e. on the issued ordinary share capital plus reserves. It therefore measures the earning capacity of the company in relation to the financial resources that have been entrusted to it by the ordinary shareholders (Table 5.1).

Table 5.1   *% Return on equity*

$$\left(\frac{pre\text{-}tax\ profit}{shareholders'\ funds} \times 100 \right)$$

	1977/ 78	1978/ 79	1979/ 80	1980/ 81	1981/ 82	1982/ 83	1983/ 84	1984/ 85	**Average 8 years**
Profit sharing companies	36.3	32.6	23.8	19.0	19.0	20.8	24.8	24.4	**25.1**
Non-profit sharing companies	30.8	27.8	20.3	13.2	12.7	14.8	19.9	19.4	**19.9**
Difference: profit sharers above (below) non-profit sharers	5.5	4.8	3.5	5.8	6.3	6.0	4.9	5.0	**5.2**

The relative performance of the profit sharers and non-profit sharers can also be illustrated graphically, as shown in Figure 5.1.

With this and other profit-related ratios, each year can be considered as a separate entity without any comparison with the preceding or subsequent years, and clearly the performance of the profit sharers, as measured by return on equity, was better than that of the non-profit sharers in every one of the eight years.

The period covered by our project included the recession of the early 1980s, and the table and graph illustrate that although the performance of both groups worsened by about the same relative degree in the first two years, the non-profit sharers slid more than the profit sharers in the depth of the recession. And although by 1985 neither group had returned to the levels of return on equity of the late 1970s, the profit sharers were somewhat ahead of the non-profit sharers.

Over the whole period the average return of the profit sharing companies was 5.2% higher than that of the non-profit sharers, which is a substantial difference. Looked at another way, the average ratio of the profit sharers at 25.1% was 26.1% above that of the non-profit sharers at 19.9%; and any company that increased its return on equity from around 20% to around 25% would almost certainly claim that its performance had improved by a quarter.

It should not be concluded, however, that every profit sharing company had a higher return on equity than any and every non-profit sharer, nor even than the average for all non-profit sharers. Some profit sharers showed a very poor performance, and some non-profit sharers a very good one. This is illustrated by the

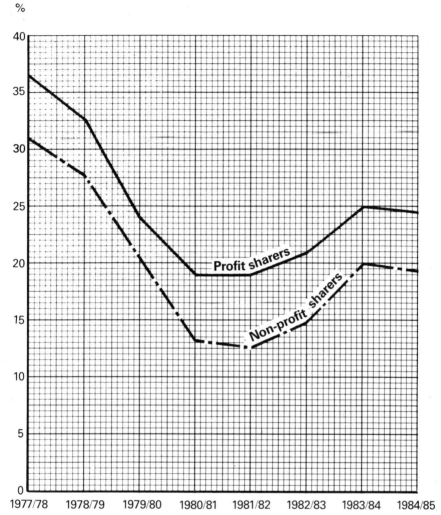

Figure 5.1 *% Return on equity*

placing of both the 113 profit sharing and the 301 non-profit sharing companies in our project in the upper half of a performance ranking table (i.e. in the top two quartiles combined) based on return on equity (Table 5.2).

Table 5.2 *Return on equity: performance ranking*

	1977/ 78	1978/ 79	1979/ 80	1980/ 81	1981/ 82	1982/ 83	1983/ 84	1984/ 85	Average 8 years
% of profit sharing companies in two top quartiles	59.8	54.9	52.2	63.7	62.8	63.1	61.8	57.7	59.5
% of non-profit sharing companies in two top quartiles	46.3	48.0	49.2	44.6	45.2	45.2	45.7	47.2	**46.4**

Consistently, a higher proportion of profit sharers than of non-profit sharers are in the upper half. It may legitimately be concluded, therefore, that profit sharing companies are rather more likely than non-profit sharers to be found in the two upper quartiles of performance as measured by return on equity.

(For other ratios the percentages of profit sharing and non-profit sharing companies in the two top quartiles are shown in Table 5.18 on page 60).

Return on capital employed

The return on capital employed (Table 5.3, Figure 5.2) is another important performance indicator, as it measures the earning ability of the company in relation to all its financial resources. It is the ratio of pre-tax profit to total net assets defined as share capital (including preference shares), plus reserves, plus creditors (long), plus any outside minority shareholdings in subsidiaries. Whereas return on equity shows how well the company performs on behalf of its ordinary shareholders, return on capital employed may be regarded as a measure of its performance on behalf of the national interest as the total resources it uses are ultimately part of our wealth as a nation.

As the same pre-tax profit is usually related to a larger base, return on capital employed is normally lower than return on equity.

Table 5.3   *% Return on capital employed*

$$\left(\frac{\text{pre-tax profit}}{\text{total net assets}} \times 100 \right)$$

	1977/ 78	1978/ 79	1979/ 80	1980/ 81	1981/ 82	1982/ 83	1983/ 84	1984/ 85	Average 8 years
Profit sharing companies	27.2	26.6	19.3	15.9	16.6	18.1	20.9	20.3	20.6
Non-profit sharing companies	22.8	20.9	16.2	10.6	10.7	12.2	15.6	15.3	15.5
Difference: profit sharers above (below) non-profit sharers	4.4	5.7	3.1	5.3	5.9	5.9	5.3	5.0	5.1

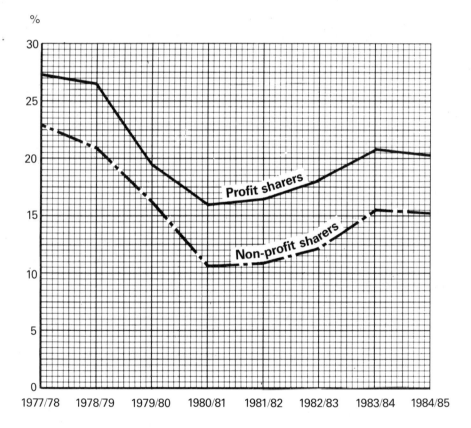

Figure 5.2   *% Return on capital employed*

These results are broadly similar to those for return on equity. The performance of the profit sharers was consistently better than that of the non-profit sharers, and their relative performance was significantly stronger during the recession: in 1980/81 the profit sharers' return was 58.5% of their 1977/78 level, whereas the non-profit sharers had fallen to 47.0%.

Over the eight years the average return of the profit sharing companies was 5.1% higher than that of the non-profit sharers, almost exactly the same as for return on equity. But the profit sharers' actual return of 20.6% was 32.9% above the 15.5% of the non-profit sharers: higher than the equivalent figure for return on equity because overall return on capital employed for both groups was about 5% lower than return on equity and so provided a lower base for comparison.

Earnings per share

Earnings per share is one of the most commonly used economic ratios in studying company performance. It is the profit attributable to ordinary shareholders (before extraordinary items) divided by the number of ordinary shares issued. As such it measures the company's performance in relation to its ordinary share capital, as distinct from return on equity which includes also reserves, and it indicates the amount per share available for reinvestment, corporation tax and dividend payments. It is therefore a performance measure that is of direct relevance to investors, and by dividing it by the dividend actually paid it indicates the dividend cover, while dividing it into the share price gives the price/earnings ratio.

Earnings per share are shown not as a percentage, but as pence per share (Table 5.4, Figure 5.3). Adjustment has been made for scrip and rights issues.

Again the results are in line with those for both return on equity and return on capital employed, which is perhaps to be expected as all three ratios show profit in relation to a capital or asset base, and with the large number of companies included in the project any individual aberrations are likely to disappear in the average. But taking the profit sharers and non-profit sharers as groups, the profit sharers had a marginally higher starting point, they withstood the depression very much better,

Table 5.4   *Earnings per share (pence)*

$$\left(\frac{profit\ attributable\ to\ ordinary\ shareholders}{number\ of\ shares\ issued}\right)$$

	1977/ 78	1978/ 79	1979/ 80	1980/ 81	1981/ 82	1982/ 83	1983/ 84	1984/ 85	Average 8 years
Profit sharing companies	14.9	17.9	15.5	14.2	14.0	15.4	19.7	18.8	16.3
Non-profit sharing companies	13.9	15.9	14.0	9.0	9.1	11.1	14.8	14.8	12.8
Difference: profit sharers above (below) non-profit sharers	1.0	2.0	1.5	5.2	4.9	4.3	4.9	4.0	3.5

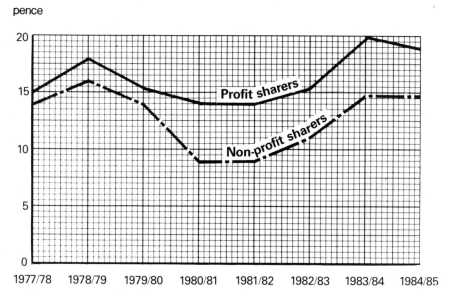

Figure 5.3   *Earnings per share (pence)*

and by the end of the period they had substantially increased their lead: in 1984/ 85 the profit sharers were 26.2% above their 1977/78 level, whereas the non-profit sharers were only 6.5% higher. And the average earnings per share of the profit sharing companies over the eight years, 16.3 pence, was 27.3% higher than the 12.8 pence of the non-profit sharing firms.

Return on sales

Return on sales, or operating margin, is the ultimate basis of profitability (Table 5.5, Figure 5.4). If a company does not make a profit on its sales, there will be no profit – unless it has a cash mountain earning interest, or disposes of or revalues assets such as property to show a paper profit. But in all normal circumstances a company's profit is derived from its sales.

Table 5.5   *% Return on sales*

$$\left(\frac{\textit{pre-tax profit}}{\textit{turnover}} \times 100 \right)$$

	1977/ 78	1978/ 79	1979/ 80	1980/ 81	1981/ 82	1982/ 83	1983/ 84	1984/ 85	Average 8 years
Profit sharing companies	10.4	10.1	8.5	6.7	7.1	7.8	8.4	8.4	8.4
Non-profit sharing companies	7.8	7.5	5.5	3.9	4.0	4.8	5.9	5.7	5.6
Difference: profit sharers above (below) non-profit sharers	2.6	2.6	3.0	2.8	3.1	3.0	2.5	2.7	2.8

This is the key to the superior performance of the profit sharing companies throughout the eight years covered by our project. A quite small difference in a company's operating margin can make a big difference to its profitability, and the profit sharers had a return 2.5% or more higher in every year. The table also shows how the profit sharers' performance was so much stronger during the recession. In 1980/81 the profit sharers' margin stood at 64.4% of its 1977/78 level, whereas the non-profit sharers' had fallen to 50%. And taking the average for the eight years, the profit sharers' margin relative to the non-profit sharers' was 50% higher. With that record, their performance on all other profit-related measures was bound to be higher.

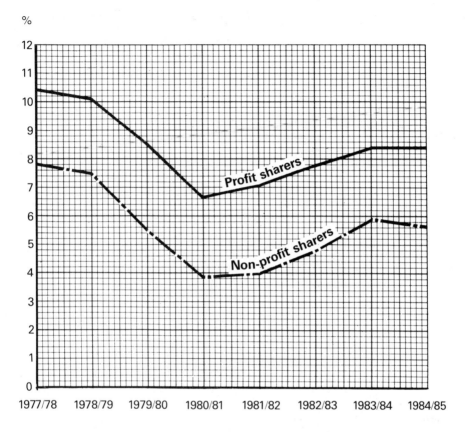

Figure 5.4   *% Return on sales*

Growth ratios

Growth in sales

We had decided that growth was important in comparing profit sharing companies with non-profit sharers. Were they more, or less, dynamic? The most obvious indication of growth is turnover, growth in sales (Table 5.6, Figure 5.5). In measuring growth, however, it is not possible to take each year as a separate entity. There must be comparison with the immediately previous year, and it was for this reason that although our project was designed to cover the eight years from 1977/78, we needed statistical information for 1976/77 as a base year. With growth ratios also, there is no second factor in the formula, as there is for profit related ratios. Thus for growth in sales, the ratio is:

sales in current year, *minus* sales in previous year (giving actual growth) *divided by* sales in the previous year (so as to express growth as a percentage).

Table 5.6   *% Annual growth in sales*
$$\left(\frac{\text{sales current year} - \text{sales previous year}}{\text{sales previous year}} \times 100\right)$$

	1977/ 78	1978/ 79	1979/ 80	1980/ 81	1981/ 82	1982/ 83	1983/ 84	1984/ 85	Average 8 years
Profit sharing companies	21.1	18.8	14.2	11.5	11.9	11.5	18.5	16.2	**15.5**
Non-profit sharing companies	18.4	19.0	14.8	8.1	10.6	11.9	14.6	12.3	**13.7**
Difference: profit sharers above (below) non-profit sharers	2.7	(0.2)	(0.6)	3.4	1.3	(0.4)	3.9	3.9	**1.8**

%

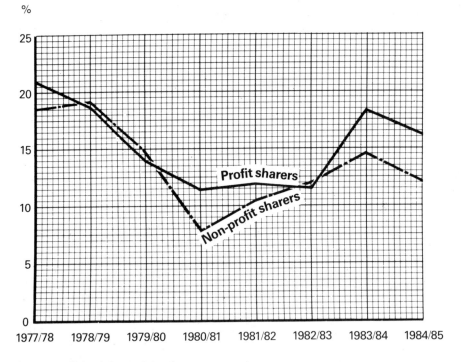

Figure 5.5   *% Annual growth in sales*

The difference between profit sharers and non-profit sharers in annual growth in sales was not nearly so dramatic as with the profit related ratios. Both groups of companies were increasing turnover at about the same pace over most of the period, with the profit sharers significantly ahead only in the last two years. But cumulative growth over the eight years is of equal interest, as is a comparison with the cumulative increase in the retail price index (Table 5.7). 1976/77 is taken as base 100 for companies' growth; December 1977 as 100 for the retail price index.

Table 5.7   *Cumulative growth in sales (%)*

	1977/ 78	1978/ 79	1979/ 80	1980/ 81	1981/ 82	1982/ 83	1983/ 84	1984/ 85
Profit sharing companies	21.1	43.9	64.3	83.2	105.0	128.6	170.8	214.7
Non-profit sharing companies	18.4	40.9	61.7	74.9	93.4	116.4	148.0	178.5
Increase in RPI	8.4	27.1	46.3	63.9	72.8	82.0	90.3	101.1

Both the profit sharing and the non-profit sharing companies had increased sales substantially above the increase in the retail price index. This indicates that growth was real, it was not just index-linked. And the profit sharing companies' cumulative growth over the eight years was significantly greater than that of the non-profit sharers.

Growth in equity

Growth in equity – the ordinary share capital plus reserves – is derived from profits which are retained in the business, plus any increase in the issued share capital (Table 5.8, Figure 5.6). It therefore measures overall growth – organic growth from within and growth by acquisitions financed by the issue of new shares.

Table 5.8 *% Annual growth in equity*

$$\left(\frac{equity\ current\ year\ -\ equity\ previous\ year}{equity\ previous\ year} \times 100 \right)$$

	1977/78	1978/79	1979/80	1980/81	1981/82	1982/83	1983/84	1984/85	Average 8 years
Profit sharing companies	29.6	24.7	16.0	21.8	11.7	12.5	14.5	10.2	**17.6**
Non-profit sharing companies	26.0	22.7	16.2	17.2	5.9	13.9	17.5	8.3	**16.0**
Difference: profit sharers above (below) non-profit sharers	3.6	2.0	(0.2)	4.6	5.8	(1.4)	(3.0)	1.9	**1.6**

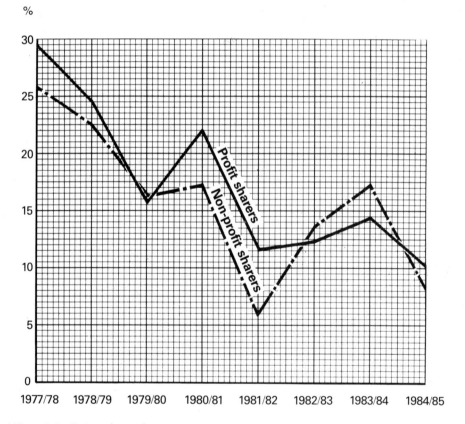

Figure 5.6 *% Annual growth in equity*

Again there was no very great difference between the profit sharing and non-profit sharing companies in their average annual growth rates, but in terms of cumulative growth (Table 5.9) the profit sharers were always in the lead, with their total growth over the eight years 38.9% more than that of the non-profit sharers.

Table 5.9 *Cumulative growth in equity (%)*
          (1976/77 base 100)

	1977/ 78	1978/ 79	1979/ 80	1980/ 81	1981/ 82	1982/ 83	1983/ 84	1984/ 85
Profit sharing companies	29.6	61.6	87.5	128.3	155.1	187.0	228.5	262.1
Non-profit sharing companies	26.0	54.6	79.6	110.5	123.0	154.0	198.4	223.2

Growth in profit

Growth in profit (Table 5.10, Figure 5.7), obviously a relevant factor in considering company performance, does not yield to the same analysis as the other ratios we have used. If all 414 companies had made a profit every year there would be no problem, but some made a loss in some years. In such cases the basis for comparison in the following year would be a negative number, and it is numerically impossible to have a negative denominator in assessing a percentage change. (Try it on your calculator!) If in year one a company made a loss of £5m, and in year two a profit of £10m, there is no way of expressing the change as a percentage of the loss (negative profit) in year one.

As our results are based on the aggregate ratios of all the profit sharing and non-profit sharing companies, therefore, we could not apply the same process to growth in profit, as to all the other ratios. Instead, for each year the total profits, minus losses, of all the profit sharing companies have been added together and divided by the number of companies, so giving the average profit for the group; similarly for the non-profit sharers. The annual growth rates are then calculated in the same way as for the other growth ratios. The reader will however recognize that with this method, changes in profits of the larger companies are given more weight than in our other calculations where it was possible to use ratios which made size irrelevant.

Table 5.10   *% Annual growth in profit*

$$\left(\frac{\text{average profit current year} - \text{average profit previous year}}{\text{average profit previous year}} \times 100\right)$$

	1977/ 78	1978/ 79	1979/ 80	1980/ 81	1981/ 82	1982/ 83	1983/ 84	1984/ 85	Average 8 years
Profit sharing companies	8.2	15.0	(12.8)	11.1	9.8	30.2	32.9	14.3	13.6
Non-profit sharing companies	9.4	6.7	(4.9)	2.9	10.2	17.6	22.3	13.7	9.7
Difference: profit sharers above (below) non-profit sharers	(1.2)	8.3	(7.9)	8.2	(0.4)	12.6	10.6	0.6	3.9

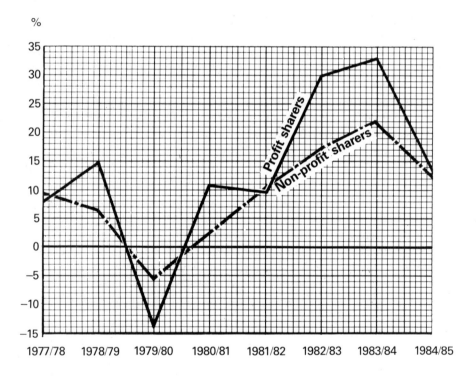

Figure 5.7   *% Annual growth in profit*

The annual rate of growth in profit, based on group averages, was very volatile for both profit sharers and non-profit sharers, but there was only one year (1979/80) when for both groups, profits were actually falling compared with the previous year. Although this shows as a negative in the table and graph, it does not mean that the companies as a group were making a loss; only that they gave up some of the increased profit they had achieved in 1978/79. This is clear from Table 5.11 showing cumulative profit growth over the eight years.

Table 5.11   *Cumulative growth in profit (%)*
             (1976/77 base 100)

	1977/ 78	1978/ 79	1979/ 80	1980/ 81	1981/ 82	1982/ 83	1983/ 84	1984/ 85
Profit sharing companies	8.2	24.4	8.5	20.5	32.4	72.3	129.0	161.8
Non-profit sharing companies	9.4	16.7	11.0	14.2	25.9	48.0	81.0	105.9

In the earlier years there is not much difference in cumulative profit growth between the two groups, but the profit sharers' generally higher annual rate of growth from 1980/81 to 1983/84 gave them a lead over the non-profit sharers for the whole period of 55.9%.

On growth ratios, therefore, as well as on the four profit-related performance ratios, the profit sharing companies as a group outperform the non-profit sharers, although not by so large a margin.

Investor returns ratios

Our final comparisons examined the two groups of companies from the point of view of the investor, the ordinary shareholder. Investors have two expectations: the expectation of income, and the expectation (or at least the hope) of capital gains. Income is derived from the dividends paid by the company; capital appreciation from any increase in the share price.

Dividends per share

We examined first the dividends paid by companies to their shareholders (Table 5.12, Figure 5.8). As with earnings per share, this is shown not as a percentage but as pence per share. Adjustment has been made for scrip and rights issues.

Table 5.12   *Dividends per share (pence)*

$$\left(\frac{total\ dividends\ paid}{number\ of\ shares\ issued}\right)$$

	1977/78	1978/79	1979/80	1980/81	1981/82	1982/83	1983/84	1984/85	Average 8 years
Profit sharing companies	3.7	4.7	5.0	4.7	4.9	5.5	6.3	6.6	5.2
Non-profit sharing companies	4.0	4.9	5.1	4.5	4.7	4.9	5.4	5.7	4.9
Difference: profit sharers above (below) non-profit sharers	(0.3)	(0.2)	(0.1)	0.2	0.2	0.6	0.9	0.9	0.3

pence

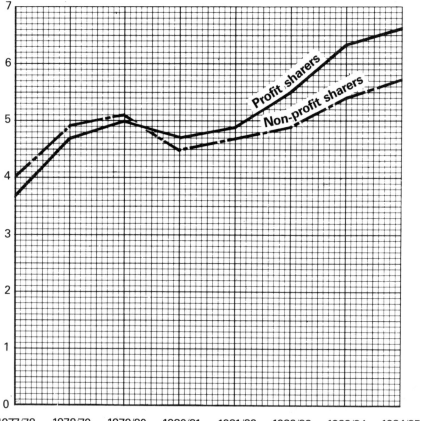

Figure 5.8   *Dividends per share (pence)*

The non-profit sharers started with higher dividend payments but gradually lost their lead and in the last three years were well below the profit sharing companies. The percentage increase for non-profit sharers in 1984/85 compared with 1977/78 was 42.5%; for profit sharers, 78.4%. Neither group managed to keep up with the percentage increase in the retail price index on the same basis (101.1%); but in 1979–1981 when, as the profit-related ratios show, companies' profits were under most strain, the RPI was rising in double figures.

Company directors usually try to maintain a progressive dividend policy, providing a steadily increasing income to their shareholders, if possible outstripping the rate of inflation, but their ability to do so depends on the profits made. It is interesting therefore to compare dividends per share with earnings per share, in terms of dividend cover (Table 5.13): the number of times the dividend is covered by earnings.

Table 5.13   *Dividend cover*

$$\left(\frac{earnings\ per\ share}{dividends\ per\ share} \right)$$

[*Dividend cover has not been calculated for each company separately. This table is derived from the group results in Table 5.4 (earnings per share) divided by the results in Table 5.12 (dividends per share)*]

	1977/ 78	1978/ 79	1979/ 80	1980/ 81	1981/ 82	1982/ 83	1983/ 84	1984/ 85	Average 8 years
Profit sharing companies	4.0	3.8	3.1	3.0	2.9	2.8	3.1	2.8	3.2
Non-profit sharing companies	3.5	3.2	2.7	2.0	1.9	2.3	2.7	2.6	2.6
Difference: profit sharers above (below) non-profit sharers	0.5	0.6	0.4	1.0	1.0	0.5	0.4	0.2	0.6

Even with the profit sharing companies apparently adopting more conservative dividend policies (maintaining a higher cover) they were still able to out-pace the non-profit sharers in the rate of increase in dividends, without reducing their dividend cover in the recession to the same degree as the non-profit sharers. This was possible only because of their superior profit performance in relation to sales, equity and capital employed. This suggests that dividends of profit sharing companies as a group are not only more likely to keep pace with inflation, but are less at risk in a recession than those of non-profit sharers. In the one year that Table 5.12 shows there was a decrease in the dividends per share for both groups (1980/81), the profit sharers dropped by only 6.0% compared with the previous year; the non-profit sharers by 11.8%.

It is relevant also that the higher the dividend cover, the more money is being ploughed back into the business, which should lead to increased profits, and the possibility of higher dividends, in future years. For investors looking for secure and increasing income, therefore, profit sharing companies appear to offer better promise than non-profit sharers; but again we must emphasize that group performance is not a dependable guide to the performance of any individual company within the group. Some profit sharers have a relatively poor dividend record; some non-profit sharers a very good one.

Total annual investor returns

Rather than analyse share price changes separately, we have taken the view that what is of interest to most investors is total return: share price variations, plus dividends (Table 5.14, Figure 5.9). This shows what, year on year, their investment has really been worth to them. The ratio is:

current year end share price, *plus* dividends received, *minus* previous year end share price (giving actual total return for the year) *divided by* previous year end share price (so as to express the change as a percentage).

The annual returns are based on calendar years. Adjustment has been made for scrip and rights issues.

Table 5.14   *Total annual investor returns (%)*

$$\left(\frac{\begin{array}{c}\textit{current year end share price plus dividends}\\ \textit{minus previous year end share price}\end{array}}{\textit{previous year end share price}} \times 100 \right)$$

	1978	1979	1980	1981	1982	1983	1984	1985	Average 8 years
Profit sharing companies	29.5	9.1	15.7	21.1	40.6	21.1	33.7	27.5	**24.8**
Non-profit sharing companies	26.9	1.5	6.0	14.6	13.4	28.4	27.6	25.9	**18.0**
Difference: profit sharers above (below) non-profit sharers	2.6	7.6	9.7	6.5	27.2	(7.4)	6.1	1.6	**6.8**

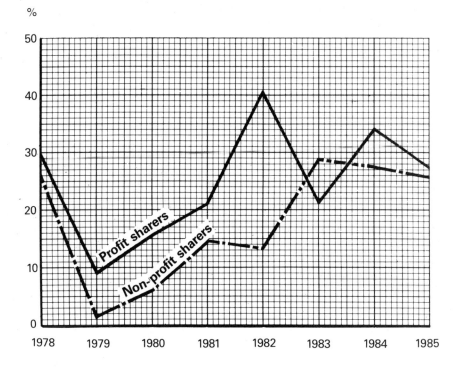

%

Figure 5.9   *Total annual investor returns (%)*

Clearly the investor who had put his money into our group of profit sharing companies on 1 January 1978 would have done much better for himself than if he had put it into the group of non-profit sharers. That of course is the wisdom of hindsight. Some of our profit sharers did not introduce schemes until later, and in most cases he would not have known that they were likely to do so. And some of both profit sharing and non-profit sharing companies that are not included in our project may have shown spectacular increases in share price by becoming the target in a takeover battle. Our selection of companies specifically required them to have full Stock Market quotations throughout the period 1976 to 1985 so takeover victims were excluded.

Nevertheless an equally weighted portfolio of shares in the profit sharing companies would have given significantly better returns, in both income growth and capital appreciation, than a similar portfolio in the non-profit sharing firms. This is illustrated by the cumulative returns that an investor would have had if he had divided his capital into equal parts among the profit sharing companies and purchased their shares on 1 January 1978, and held them, with all dividends being reinvested in the same companies, until 31 December in any year up to and including 1985, compared with dividing the same capital sum into equal parts among the non-profit sharers on the same basis (Table 5.15).

Table 5.15   *Cumulative investor returns (%)*
             (1 January 1978 – 31 December 1985)

	1978	1979	1980	1981	1982	1983	1984	1985
Profit sharing companies	29.5	41.3	63.5	98.0	178.3	236.8	350.3	474.1
Non-profit sharing companies	26.9	28.8	36.5	56.5	77.4	127.8	190.7	266.0

If he had kept his investments for the whole of the eight years his total returns from the profit sharing companies would have been 78.2% more than from the non-profit sharers. Looked at another way, £10 000 divided among the non-profit sharers would have become £36 600; divided among the profit sharers it would have become £57 410.

Before and after

Of our 113 profit sharing companies 48 had schemes which first came into operation in 1980/81. For these companies we examined their performance before and after the schemes started, and compared it with the performance of all 301 non-profit sharers for the same periods (Table 5.16). So as not to cause confusion by presenting too many statistics we show only the difference by which the performance of these 48 profit sharing companies was above, or below, that of the non-profit sharers, for the average of the four years 1977/78–1980/81 before, and the four years 1981/82–1984/85 after their schemes had started.

From this it is clear that in relation to the non-profit sharing companies, these late-starting profit sharers had for all except two ratios maintained or increased the lead they had already established in the first four years, in the last four after their schemes were fully operative. 'After' is rather better than 'before'.

Table 5.16   *Before and after the introduction of profit sharing. The performance of the group of 48 companies which introduced profit sharing in 1980/81, compared with the group of 301 non-profit sharers*

	Difference: profit sharing companies above (below) non-profit sharers, for average of four years, 1977/78 – 1980/81	Difference: profit sharing companies above (below) non-profit sharers, for average of four years, 1981/82 – 1984/85
% Return on equity	5.3	5.6
% Return on capital employed	5.4	5.4
Earnings per share (pence)	2.4	2.4
% Return on sales	2.6	1.7
% Annual growth in sales	3.3	5.2
% Annual growth in equity	2.9	3.1
% Annual growth in profit	8.7	(0.4)
Dividends per share (pence)	(0.5)	0.2
% Total annual investor returns	9.1	10.3

Conclusion

Summary of results

In this chapter we have presented the main findings of our project. These have shown that the economic performance of profit sharing companies taken as a group was superior by a significant degree to that of non-profit sharers as a group in terms of profitability, growth and investor returns. To present the results in summary, Table 5.17 shows how the performance of the group of 113 profit sharing firms compared with, and surpassed, that of the group of 301 non-profit sharers over the eight years 1977/78 to 1984/85.

Table 5.17 *Summary: comparative performance of profit sharing and non-profit sharing companies*

Average ratios for eight years 1977/78–1984/85		Profit sharing companies	Non-profit sharing companies	Actual difference: profit sharers above non-profit sharers	% difference: profit sharers above non-profit sharers
Profitability ratios	Return on equity (%)	25.1	19.9	5.2	26.1
	Return on capital employed (%)	20.6	15.5	5.1	32.9
	Earnings per share (pence)	16.3	12.8	3.5	27.3
	Return on sales (%)	8.4	5.6	2.8	50.0
Growth ratios	Annual growth in sales (%)	15.5	13.7	1.8	13.1
	Annual growth in equity (%)	17.6	16.0	1.6	10.0
	Annual growth in profit (%)	13.6	9.7	3.9	40.2
Investor returns	Dividends per share (pence)	5.2	4.9	0.3	6.1
ratios	Total annual returns (%)	24.8	18.0	6.8	37.8
Cumulative growth, eight years					
	Growth in sales(%)	214.7	178.5	36.2	20.3
	Growth in equity (%)	262.1	223.2	38.9	17.4
	Growth in profit (%)	161.8	105.9	55.9	52.8
	Total investor returns(%)	474.1	266.0	208.1	78.2

In this summary we show the difference between the profit sharers and the non-profit sharers in two modes so as to meet the needs of analysts who may wish to interpret them in different ways. First is the actual difference, e.g. the profit sharers' return on equity was 5.2% higher than that of the non-profit sharers. But this represents a relative margin of 26.1% over the non-profit sharers' return of 19.2%, and this is shown in the last column.

We point out, however, that the relative margin depends not only on the actual difference, but on the base with which it is compared. Thus an actual difference of only 2.8% return on sales (substantial though that is in trading terms) gives a relative margin of 50% when compared with the base for non-profit sharers of 5.6%.

Our findings also show that for most of the ratios the profit sharers maintained or increased their relative lead over the eight years, and that although both groups of companies were severely affected by the recession in the early 1980s, its effect on the non-profit sharing companies was significantly greater than on the profit sharers.

Performance ranking

Finally, the percentages of both profit sharers and non-profit sharers in the top two quartiles of performance ranking tables for each ratio are shown in Table 5.18 (overleaf). (Growth in profit is excluded as it could not be analysed on a comparable basis as a ratio.)

This shows that for all the profitability and growth ratios, more than half of the profit sharing companies were in the top two quartiles in every year, and more than half of the non-profit sharers were in the bottom two. For dividends per share the same was true except in the first two years, and for total annual investor returns, except in three years.

On this evidence, profit sharers as a group rank higher in all the performance tables than non-profit sharers, and profit sharing companies are more likely than non-profit sharers to be found in the two upper quartiles. This also demonstrates that the higher group averages of the profit sharing companies for all ratios as summarized in Table 5.17 are the result of their superior performance as a group and not due to exceptional results from just a few companies.

These are objective observations based on the statistical analysis. In the next chapter we consider some of the factors that help to make profit sharing companies more profitable.

Table 5.18 *Performance ranking: percentages of profit sharing and non-profit sharing companies in the top two quartiles*

		1977/ 78	1978/ 79	1979/ 80	1980/ 81	1981/ 82	1982/ 83	1983/ 84	1984/ 85	Average 8 years
Return on equity	Profit sharing companies	59.8	54.9	52.2	63.7	62.8	63.1	61.8	57.7	59.5
	Non-profit sharing companies	46.3	48.0	49.2	44.6	45.2	45.2	45.7	47.2	46.4
Return on capital employed	Profit sharing companies	60.7	60.2	54.9	61.9	64.6	64.9	64.5	55.8	60.9
	Non-profit sharing companies	45.4	46.1	48.1	45.3	44.5	44.5	44.7	47.9	45.8
Earnings per share	Profit sharing companies	51.4	61.1	63.6	62.0	63.9	62.3	63.9	61.2	61.2
	Non-profit sharing companies	49.3	45.2	44.3	45.3	44.5	44.9	44.8	45.7	45.5
Return on sales	Profit sharing companies	66.4	68.1	65.5	68.1	69.0	68.5	69.6	65.4	67.6
	Non-profit sharing companies	43.5	42.7	44.1	43.2	42.9	43.2	42.7	44.2	43.3
Growth in sales	Profit sharing companies	59.8	55.8	52.2	64.6	63.7	63.1	63.6	54.8	59.7
	Non-profit sharing companies	46.3	47.6	49.2	44.5	44.9	45.2	45.0	48.2	46.4
Growth in equity	Profit sharing companies	58.9	58.4	50.4	61.9	61.9	59.5	57.3	54.8	57.9
	Non-profit sharing companies	46.6	46.3	49.7	45.5	45.2	46.5	47.2	48.2	46.9
Dividends per share	Profit sharing companies	44.3	47.2	52.7	50.5	50.0	55.9	56.7	55.6	51.6
	Non-profit sharing companies	51.3	48.4	47.0	49.2	49.4	46.3	45.4	46.5	47.9
Total investor returns*	Profit sharing companies	48.5	57.3	60.2	61.2	61.2	46.6	52.4	46.7	54.3
	Non-profit sharing companies	50.4	46.9	45.8	45.4	45.4	51.2	48.8	51.2	48.1

*Total investor returns are for calendar years 1978 to 1985

CHAPTER 6

Profit sharing and participative management

The economic performance of a group of 113 UK quoted profit sharing companies was on average significantly better than the equivalent performance of a comparable group of 301 non-profit sharing companies over the period 1978–1985: that is what has been demonstrated in Chapter 5. But why? To say it is because they are profit sharing is simply to re-state the problem without answering the question. Profit sharing companies must possess certain other characteristics, or have some characteristics more strongly developed than in non-profit sharers, that account for, or contribute to, their greater success.

We suggest there are two sets of such characteristics. The first are those that actually lead a company to introduce profit sharing rather than remain a non-profit sharer. The second are characteristics that are developed largely as a result of its being a profit sharer. Both are associated with the style of management of the company.

What makes one company more successful than another is normally the quality of its management. A badly managed company is very unlikely to be successful, except in the short term if luck happens to be on its side. A well-managed company is likely to be relatively successful even in adversity.

Good managers usually have clear and defined objectives and the ability to harness all the resources necessary to achieve them.* They recognize that their most important resource is people, and they know that people are different in kind from all the other resources they use. Whereas materials and machinery respond mechanistically and separately to the way they are treated, people respond emotionally, and often collectively, and that is a very different thing. It is relatively

---

*The 'Statement of company objectives' of H.P. Bulmer Holdings PLC is a good example. It is reproduced on pages 68–69

easy to get optimum results from materials and machinery. Use them for their proper purpose, ensure they are maintained in good condition, do not subject them to undue strain, and little more is needed.

Many managers have traditionally treated people in much the same way. They have regarded people as just another commodity, as 'hands' to be bought in as cheaply as possible and put to work in the same way as plant or machinery. And when people – employees – reacted by doing as little work as possible, and showing no concern for the quality of their product, management in turn reacted by increasing supervision and tightening up the rules. It was their one concession to recognizing that people were different, but they saw the difference in terms of inherent obstinacy and a propensity for conflict. People were unfortunately less tractable than things. With people it was 'them and us', and all the blame was attributed to 'them'.

Employees seen as co-partners

A very different management style was reflected in the philosophy of the nineteenth century profit sharing or co-partnership firms. The founders of those firms saw labour not as a commodity, a cost of production, but as employees who were co-partners with managers and owners, all working together for, and sharing in, the success and prosperity of the enterprise. This philosophy is manifested in a practical way today in companies that prepare their accounts, or at least their internal accounts, so as to show value added or wealth created. To them 'costs' are the cost of bought in materials and bought in services (rates, energy, interest on loans and so on). But payroll is not shown as a cost. On the other side of the balance is sales; and the difference between costs and sales is the value that the company has added to the bought in goods and services by its processes of manufacture and distribution. And the parties who are shown as sharing the value added are employees (through payroll), the company itself (through retained profit), shareholders (through dividends) and the community (through corporation and payroll taxes). (Depreciation – the cost of replacing equipment – is sometimes shown as a cost, sometimes as part of value added.)

In non-manufacturing industries 'value added' may not be an appropriate measure but even using a different yardstick the basic concept is the same. It reflects a fundamentally different view of the place of employees in the company, compared with the adversarial concept of 'them and us'. Employees are seen as part of, and partners in, the enterprise. Whether or not the accounts are presented in a value added format, this view of employees by management is one of the characteristics of most profit sharing companies and one of the factors that originally will have led them to become profit sharers.

That is not to say that the same attitude will not also be found among many non-profit sharing firms. Good and enlightened management is not confined to the profit sharers, and there are undoubtedly many non-profit sharing companies whose managements regard employees as by far their most important resource, and whose approach to them is on a basis of working together rather than inherent conflict. But the adversarial management approach is fundamentally incompatible with the philosphy of profit sharing. Thus we would expect that among profit sharing companies as a group there will be a high concentration of partnership or cooperative managements, whereas the adversarialists will tend to be concentrated among the non-profit sharers.

Employee attitudes

A partnership approach by management is, however, of itself not a sufficient basis for a company to adopt profit sharing. Without it, profit sharing is unlikely, but even with it, more is needed. Managers may regard employees as partners in the enterprise, but that will achieve little unless they are able, to some degree at least, to generate a reciprocal attitude among the employees themselves. The adversarial approach is by no means a management prerogative. 'Them and us' attitudes are found equally, and sometimes even more strongly, among employees towards management. But the initiative in overcoming them must come from management.

What, from the point of view of employees, is the basis of 'them and us'? We suggest there are three main ingredients: (a) a distrust of what management tells them; (b) the belief that management is out to exploit the workforce, to 'do us down'; and (c) the concept of privilege, that 'they' are different from 'us'.

(a) Distrust, it must be said, has in very many instances been justified. The only way one can hope to dispel it is by management providing information, both on its own initiative and in response to questions, consistently, regularly, openly and in sufficient detail, so that over time people begin to see for themselves that what management tells them is in fact true. To achieve this will take a great deal of painstaking effort over a long period. Management has to prove that it can be trusted. And it requires constant vigilance. Trust may take months, even years, to establish. It can be destroyed in less than a minute. Trust does not mean that everyone will necessarily like, or agree with, what they are told: at times they may vehemently oppose it. But it does imply an acceptance that management is being honest with them.

(b) Similarly it may take just as much effort to overcome the belief that management will always try to exploit the workforce. It will require real and open discussion of issues affecting pay, conditions, the workload and working practices and so on. This is not the place to examine the various participative arrangements and processes that may be appropriate for such discussion, but if other circumstances are favourable, this is an area where profit sharing may be relevant.*

---

*For examples of good practice in participative management see the case studies in Part III of *Participation Today* by Rex Adams, Industrial Participation Association, 1984

It is evidence of good faith if management is prepared to introduce a meaningful profit sharing scheme and open the books to show how the bonus is determined.

(c) The idea of privilege, and that they (managers) are different from us (employees), is less tangible and perhaps can never be entirely dispelled. But there are some things that may exacerbate and some that may mitigate it. It is not usually a question of jealousy: most employees do not begrudge senior managers having high salaries and expensive company cars if they feel that they are doing a good job (although salaries that read like telephone numbers may be looked at askance).

Among the mitigating factors are such things as common terms and conditions of employment (the same working week for everyone, the same holiday entitlement, sickness benefit and so on); one pension scheme with the same terms for all staff; everyone using the same staff restaurant; and a range of other 'equalizers' depending on circumstances and practicality. In essence the guiding principle should be to avoid as far as possible all unnecessary status and other differentials apart from pay. But even more important in our view is the manner in which managers at all levels actually treat the people for whom they are responsible, and how senior managers treat employees generally. The manager who regularly (daily) walks the works and has a friendly word with everyone, who is accessible when needed and who discusses with, rather than simply tells people what has to be done, will go a long way to break down the barriers of 'difference'.

In visiting a factory or office for the first time it usually takes no more than two minutes to sense what the atmosphere is like. There is a different spirit about in what we would describe as the participative company, and it very quickly becomes apparent.

This then is another characteristic of most profit sharing companies: an erosion of the 'them and us' barriers not only on the part of managers, but among employees generally. It may be the result of a deliberate and considered management policy; it may be simply because that is the way the company's managers find it natural to manage, and their attitude generates a reciprocal response from the workforce. Again it is not unique to profit sharing firms but it is one of the factors that, other things being equal, may move a company towards profit sharing.

Generating commitment to success

The third characteristic conducive to the introduction of profit sharing is management's recognition that for a company to be really successful it needs the commitment of all its employees. It is only when everyone is pulling together that the best results can be achieved.

There are many ways of generating commitment and again this book is not the place to examine them all, but clearly one of the most effective must be by linking the interests of employees – especially their financial interests – with the interests of the company. If the employees believe that all the benefits of success are going to others – the shareholders, the senior managers – why should they care? As one managing director put it, 'it really is rather silly talking to employees about profit if they don't get any of it'.

If therefore these three attributes are present: management regarding employees as part of, and partners in, the enterprise; their having generated a reciprocal attitude among employees; and there being an overall commitment to success, the conditions are propitious for the introduction of profit sharing. If they are not present, management is much less likely to think that profit sharing would be worth while.

Impact of profit sharing

The features that are commonly developed in companies as a result of profit sharing are largely an extension of those characteristics that led to its introduction in the first place. They relate to the provision of information, the perceived credibility of management, openness as far as possible about the company's plans and prospects, and cooperation in improving performance. A profit sharing company cannot be run as a secret society. If management is serious about profit sharing, one of its objectives will be to encourage employees to take a greater interest in the company's financial results. But that can only be achieved if employees are given – and know they can trust – the relevant figures. And they should be able directly to relate their actual or prospective profit sharing bonuses to those figures.

Profit sharing companies therefore usually provide a great deal of financial information to their employees. (Sometimes perhaps too much: the art is to keep the presentations clear and simple, and not to bombard people with masses of detailed statistics that neither they nor most of their managers can comprehend.) As profits are derived from sales to customers, information is also provided about such things as the order book, work schedules and delivery dates, repeat orders, changing markets – and the competition. The aim is to make employees customer-conscious: in Conder Group, which has a long established profit sharing scheme, in the entrance to every plant there is prominently displayed a bust of 'The Satisfied Customer – the most important person in our business'.

Such a free flow of information can lead to discussion of ways of improving quality, cost saving, new working methods and new technology: all the things that will help the company to keep in the forefront of its industry and secure its future. This is not simply management talking to the workforce. Through workgroup discussions, project teams, working parties, productivity committees, it is attempting to tap the resources of knowledge and skills of people at every level that are so often neglected, and to harness their energy in cooperation with management in improving performance. And the readiness of people to take part in such activities, and contribute to them, will be enhanced by their knowledge that through profit sharing they themselves will be directly benefiting from the results of any improvements.

There will often also be some special forum such as a company council where future plans, new investment and employment prospects can be discussed. But as management knows that even with the best will in the world sometimes things will go wrong, people will be upset, grievances will occur, the profit sharing company will usually have some effective way of detecting and dealing with such problems at an early stage before they can escalate into major disturbances.

Management's accountability

By involving employees in these ways, and encouraging them to take an interest in the business and in improving its performance, management has to be prepared for questions and criticism. Participative management does not mean management by committee, or joint decision making. Managers remain responsible for making the decisions within the area of their own accountability, but in the participative company they will make many of those decisions having first sought, and taken account of, the views of the people for whom they are responsible; and they will often make better decisions as a result, because some of their original ideas will have been modified and improved by the suggestions of those whom they have consulted. And having taken a decision, they must be prepared to explain it, especially if it has gone against the views put forward by employees.

Again through profit sharing, employees have a personal interest in the quality of decision making in their company. Their willingness to cooperate in improving performance would soon evaporate if they felt that all their efforts were being frustrated by bad decisions on the part of management. Profit sharing, if carried through so as to encourage everyone in the organization to be more profit-conscious, therefore requires a more open management style, and a greater accountability for decision making. There is likely to be much less talk of 'management's right to manage', but more of, what in reality is the case, 'management's responsibility to manage.'

It would however be unrealistic to suggest that all these characteristics are to be found in all profit sharing companies. No two companies are alike and each will have its own configuration of management style and employee involvement. Sometimes it will vary at different levels in the organization, or in different departments or locations, and some companies will not be successful in some of the things they attempt. Nor are any of the features of employee involvement that are generally characteristic of profit sharing companies confined to the profit sharers. All of them will be found, in one form or another, in many non-profit sharing organizations. But they are more likely to be found, and likely to be more effective, among the profit sharers.

Profit sharing gives management a better opportunity to talk to employees about the business, its performance, its profitability, its prospects, because people are naturally more interested when they know they have a personal stake in its success. And for the same reason employees in a profit sharing company are that much more ready to help in improving its performance. So with profit sharing, participation comes full circle. It is the more participative companies that are most likely to introduce profit sharing; and as a consequence of profit sharing, those companies are likely to become even more participative.

There are of course exceptions. Everyone will be able to give an example of a particular profit sharing company that is notoriously unsuccessful or has an appalling record of industrial relations. But one will usually find that in such a company profit sharing was introduced for the wrong motives – perhaps for political reasons, or because it was seen to be fashionable, but without any genuine commitment by top management to employee involvement. In those circumstances profit sharing will do nothing to alleviate what may be an already bad situation. Profit sharing of itself will not change a management style. Management's commitment has to come first, and must be the basis for the further development of employee involvement through the profit sharing scheme, otherwise both managers and employees are likely soon to become disillusioned.

Tax concessions

This is the reason for our one reservation about tax concessions intended to encourage the spread of profit sharing. By giving the stamp of government approval, linked with a financial incentive, tax concessions may induce some companies to introduce profit sharing when they are not ready for it. In many of the most successful profit sharing firms management has said that profit sharing was introduced only when they had already made good progress towards a more participative management, and in the development of effective employee involvement. Profit sharing then stands on its own merits; it does not need, or depend on, tax concessions.

If tax concessions tip the balance by encouraging firms that are potentially ready for profit sharing to introduce it, that is to be welcomed. And if they enable such firms, and others that already have established schemes, to offer their employees a greater benefit by taking their bonus in the form of shares rather than cash, again, but for different reasons, it is to be welcomed. But if they were to lead to the introduction of profit sharing in firms where it would be totally inconsistent with the overall style of management, with all parties locked into strongly adversarial attitudes, then it could conceivably worsen relations and fuel existing tensions.

In general, however, profit sharing companies not only have a very good record of industrial relations, but they exhibit many, and often most, of the characteristics of management style and employee involvement that we have described in this chapter. And as these characteristics are more commonly found in profit sharing companies than in non-profit sharers (because they lead companies to introduce profit sharing, and are further developed as a result) we believe this goes far to explain the superior economic performance of profit sharing firms compared with non-profit sharers as demonstrated by our project.

We do not claim therefore that the results discussed in Chapter 5 show that profit sharing by itself leads to improved profitability. That would be altogether too simplistic a conclusion. Rather we believe that profit sharing is normally a consequence of the participative style set by the top management in a company; and that it is this management style, with profit sharing as one of the keys to generating commitment to the firm's success, that produces the handsome return for shareholders, managers and employees alike that is demonstrated in our findings.

The following 'Statement of company objectives' is quoted with permission from the Annual Report and Accounts for 1985/86 of H.P. Bulmer Holdings PLC, the world's largest cider-maker:

H.P. Bulmer Holdings PLC and subsidiaries
Statement of company objectives

We believe that success in any company can be achieved only if every employee understands and supports the objectives which the company, and each individual in it, is striving to attain. Each year we review and, after consultation with the Employee Council, where necessary revise them.

These objectives are not necessarily of equal importance and at different times some may require more attention than others.

1. To increase profitability and earnings per share each year by improving our added value (the amount which remains after the cost of materials and bought-in services has been deducted from sales income).

2. To continue to make and sell products of high quality and to give the utmost consideration to the needs and interests of our customers.

3. To pay the best wages and salary rates we can afford, and to ensure job satisfaction for all employees through enlightened management. To improve working conditions wherever possible and to take all appropriate steps to ensure the health and safety of all employees. To promote the best possible human relations and a situation in which people really enjoy working for the company.

4. To remain an independent public company with a distinctive style.

5. To give executives the maximum freedom of action, and to encourage them to make the fullest use of it, so that they can personally influence profits.

6. To continue to encourage employee share ownership in the company.

7. To encourage participation by keeping employees informed of policy, progress and problems, to invite comments and criticisms and to show everyone how individual effort contributes to the company's success.

8. To be flexible and not to depend too much on any one product, customer or market. Whilst retaining our leading position in the cider and pectin markets, to continue to broaden the base of the trading activities of the group at home and overseas. To maintain an efficient research and development policy so that opportunities can be quickly recognized and speedily exploited.

9. To promote job security and to avoid compulsory redundancy by careful forward planning and by the early recognition of the effects of change.

10. To train and develop all employees and to promote from within whenever possible.

11. To ensure the economical supply of our vital raw materials.

12. To benefit the local community whenever and wherever the group can afford to do so, and to preserve the quality of life and of the environment.

CHAPTER 7

Introducing a profit sharing scheme

Managements which are considering the introduction of profit sharing into their companies should first examine their motivation in doing so, and their objectives. For many in the past, the main motivation was what has been described as the inherent rightness of profit sharing – that employees should have a share of the profit they have helped to generate, the wealth they have helped to create. And linked with that was the desire to strengthen the sense of identity of all employees with the company for which they work.

These are principles which are still fundamental to the success of any profit sharing scheme, and most other objectives derive from them, but management should consider whether there are any more specific objectives they also wish to achieve. Some of the other common objectives in profit sharing were mentioned in Chapter 1, such as:

- to enable employees to build up a personal stake in the company through share ownership;
- to encourage them to take more interest in the company's profitability and results;
- to encourage employees generally to consider whether they could do more to contribute to the firm's success;
- to attract and retain staff.

The list is by no means exhaustive! But the design of a scheme that will be most appropriate for the company will depend both on what are management's motivation and objectives, and on whether those objectives are realistically attainable in the particular circumstances of the company itself.

Here the first and most important question is, will it fit in with the underlying philosophy and general style of management of the company? Is top management committed to the participative style of management that is needed for profit sharing to be worthwhile? And is it prepared to ensure that this runs through the management chain generally? As one chief executive put it, 'In this company participation is voluntary on the shop floor, but for management it is mandatory'. Unless therefore top management is satisfied that these conditions prevail, it would be much better to postpone profit sharing and concentrate on doing something about the management style; or if that is not seen as practicable or desirable, forget about profit sharing altogether.

Management should also consider how profit sharing would fit in with any other financial participation schemes in the company – special bonus schemes for some groups of employees, share option schemes and so on. It is essential that profit sharing should be seen to be fair, and if it were to give substantial extra benefits to a minority of employees who already enjoy a highly geared remuneration package, but little to the majority at the lower end of the pay scale, it could cause resentment rather than satisfaction. This again is something that has to be taken into account in the design of an appropriate scheme. (We discuss profit sharing in relation to share option schemes in the following chapter.)

The next question should be, can the company afford to have a profit sharing scheme? And associated with this, how much money is it prepared to put into it? Management will have to accept that in the first years it is money that is unlikely to produce any immediate return. We believe that the long-term effect of profit sharing as a key element in management's efforts to secure commitment to the firm's success will be beneficial – and the record of the profit sharing companies' performance as demonstrated by our project reinforces that belief – but it will not happen overnight. The time scale will vary from company to company, but we suggest that for most it will probably be two or three years before profit sharing begins to have any real impact. Even then its effect may not be measurable. Any improvement in the company's performance will be the result of a number of factors, and it will be difficult to quantify how much is directly attributable to profit sharing.

Generally speaking, the less money per employee that goes into the scheme, the less effect it is likely to have. With very small amounts, the impact may even be negative if the scheme is regarded as derisory by most employees – a profit sharing bonus of £100 a year to someone earning £10 000 will not generate much enthusiasm. In schemes with cash bonuses, a minimum of 4% or 5% of annual salary in a normal trading year should be the target, with the possibility of the bonus rising to 10% or more in very good years, or shrinking to zero in very bad ones. In share-based schemes, where there is no immediate cash benefit, it may perhaps be a little lower, but we would still regard a minimum of 4% or so in a normal year as desirable.

Clearly it will be more difficult – or more costly – for a scheme to provide worthwhile bonuses in a labour-intensive industry with low profit margins, and this again is something that must be taken into account first in deciding whether or not any scheme is practicable, and if so, in its design. It is relevant to note here that the Investment Protection Committees representing pension funds and insurance companies have issued guidelines for publicly quoted companies indicating that not more than 5% of a company's pre-tax trading profit should go into an all-employee profit sharing scheme. Most major companies observe that limit; a few do not, and a number of private companies allocate a much higher proportion of profit to their schemes.

Cash or shares?

We have so far discussed the issues that should determine whether or not any form of profit sharing is appropriate for the company. If management decides that it is, the next question is whether it should be a cash scheme, a share-based scheme, or one giving employees the choice between cash and shares.

For some companies, only a cash scheme will be practicable. This will be the case for subsidiaries where the parent is not willing, or not able, to have a share-based scheme, or if the parent company, for example a large conglomerate, is so remote from employees in the subsidiary that its shares would seem of little relevance to them. It will also apply if the share performance of the parent may have no relation to, or even move counter to, the profit performance of the subsidiary. For many private companies also, cash schemes will be more practicable. (We discuss later the special considerations relevant to private firms.)

In any company a cash scheme is likely to have a more immediate impact than one based on shares. Cash in hand once or twice a year or even more frequently will be seen as more directly related to profit (or whatever other measure of performance is used as the basis for the scheme) than a *proforma* certificate indicating that so many shares have been appropriated to trustees in the employee's name, that is received some months after the end of the financial year to which it relates. If therefore one of the main objectives of the scheme is to encourage discussion about ways of improving performance, and management intends to provide regular monthly or quarterly progress reports showing what has been achieved, a cash scheme is probably the most appropriate.

A share-based scheme, on the other hand, may have greater long-term impact by strengthening the sense of identity with the company, because employees not only get an annual bonus related to profit, but they have a personal stake, even if a small one, in ownership; and if they retain their shares, as apparently most do, it will be an increasing stake. If therefore increasing the sense of identity is a main objective, and if a share scheme is practicable, that will be the best choice. Because of the tax concessions in the Finance Act 1978, a share scheme will also provide employees with bonuses of greater value than a cash scheme, and if new shares are issued for the share appropriation, there will be some benefit to the company's cash flow.

(That may be a marginal reason for choosing a share scheme rather than cash, but not for deciding on profit sharing in the first instance.)

If employees are given the choice between taking the bonus in cash or in shares, it must be expected that the majority at shop-floor level will probably choose cash. For most people a bird in the hand (even a smaller taxed one) is still worth two in the bush. It is the higher paid employees on higher marginal tax rates who are more likely to choose shares. Almost all the companies in which there is such a choice originally had cash schemes in place before 1978. A Finance Act approved scheme was later introduced in parallel to allow employees who wished to take advantage of the tax concessions to do so by taking shares rather than cash. Few entirely new schemes allow the choice.

Who should participate?

Probably the next question is, who should participate? And the best answer, everyone. Profit sharing should be a unifying factor in a company, not a divisive one. If possible, therefore, all employees should be included. With cash schemes this is a realistic possibility; even new recruits can participate, *pro rata* to their length of service, from the day they join the company. It is however a reasonable stipulation that the employee must still be with the company when the bonus is actually paid, although in many schemes involuntary leavers (because of retirement, injury, illness, possibly redundancy) participate *pro rata* to the date when they leave.

Despite our saying 'everyone', if directors or senior executives already have profit-related bonuses on top of their basic salaries it may be considered whether or not they should benefit additionally from an all-employee scheme. In some companies also, other employees in productivity or other bonus schemes are included in the profit sharing scheme but at a reduced rate. And in labour-intensive industries, if the inclusion of all employees would be likely to reduce individual bonuses to a derisory level, it may be necessary to reduce numbers by having a length of service qualification – for example, that employees begin to participate only when they have completed two years service with the company.

With a cash scheme, or indeed any scheme that does not require Inland Revenue approval, management can in fact decide just who should participate, and at what level. There are no constraints other than the moral one that the scheme should be seen as fair, and what is practicable in the circumstances of the company. In a share-based scheme operating under the provisions of the Finance Act 1978, however, all full-time UK employees, including directors, who have completed five years continuous service with the company must be included. Management can decide what other employees to include as well, and the same principle applies – as far as possible, everyone. In most schemes regular part-timers are included, and the length of service qualification is between one and three years rather than five; in some, the only requirement is that the participant was employed by the company throughout the relevant financial year and is still in its employment when the shares are appropriated to the trustees of the scheme. But as with cash schemes, in labour-intensive industries it may be necessary to have a longer service qualification in order to provide worthwhile bonuses for those who do participate.

With a share scheme also, it is worth considering the normal pattern of labour turnover in the company. It is not really worth the administrative hassle of making a single allocation of shares to a large number of employees if a high proportion of them are likely to leave during the following year. In many firms there is a critical point up to which labour turnover is high, but beyond which the record shows that most employees are likely to remain for some considerable time. That point is probably right for the length of service qualification to participate in a share-based profit sharing scheme.

In an approved share scheme all eligible employees must participate 'on similar terms'. This does not mean that everyone must receive the same number of shares (although that is possible) but it does prevent management from deciding that some groups, such as those benefiting from other bonus schemes, should participate in the profit sharing scheme at a reduced rate. In a few companies with long-established schemes which had such differential rates for different groups of employees, and in which a Finance Act scheme has been introduced in parallel, the approved scheme therefore operates only at the lowest rate of participation, and those enjoying a higher rate must receive their additional bonus outside the approved scheme, and subject to income tax deduction. While it would technically be possible for an entirely new scheme to have similar two-tier levels of participation, with only the lower one operating within the approved scheme, in normal circumstances we would not recommend it. There are circumstances, however, in which some or even all employees may have to receive part of their bonus either in cash or in shares outside an approved scheme and subject to PAYE deduction. This will happen if the scheme formula produces bonuses in excess of the limits currently laid down for approved share schemes (at present £1250 or 10% of salary up to an overall maximum of £5000).

Basis of distribution

In any profit sharing scheme a major consideration is the basis on which employees should participate. There are schemes in which the formula automatically determines the bonus as a percentage of salary, but most scheme formulae produce a total bonus fund which then has to be divided among the eligible employees. There are basically three possibilities:

- proportionate to salary;
- equal shares for all;
- related to length of service.

A survey of profit sharing and employee shareholding schemes in 1980 showed that in 70% of all schemes the bonus was proportionate to salary.* The reasoning is that the relative value of employees' contributions to the business is reflected in their salaries, and they should therefore receive the same relative share of any profit sharing fund. But a supplementary question then is, what salary? Should it be basic salary on a given date, or total annual earnings? Or if all staff are graded, should all in the same grade receive the same amount? Here there is no best answer; every company must decide for itself.

The case for equal shares for all is that employees' contributions to the enterprise are already fully rewarded by their wages or salaries, but as the smooth running and success of the business depend ultimately on the cooperation of everyone in it, whatever is available as profit sharing over and above their proper remuneration should be equally divided among them all.

When length of service is taken into account it is usually as a multiplier, either of equal shares for all, or of bonuses first calculated proportionate to salary. But if a length of service factor is applied, it should not be such as to produce very high bonuses for long-serving, highly paid staff, out of all proportion to those of lower paid employees with only a few years service. From our experience we consider that a multiplier of 1.5 should be the maximum.

It is worth considering some sophistication of an otherwise simple formula. For example, in the first instance to use the total fund to provide an equal bonus of up to, say, £200 for everyone, any extra then being allocated proportionate to salary; or to put an upper limit on the amount of salary that is eligible for bonus. These and many other variations have been used by different companies, and provided they apply across the board (so that everyone participates on similar terms) are acceptable for schemes approved under the provisions of the 1978 Finance Act.

A few companies have in the past attempted to use profit sharing as a disciplinary tool by withholding all or part of the bonus of employees who had been absent, late, taken part in industrial action, or otherwise incurred management's opprobrium. Others have used it as a reward mechanism by increasing the bonus allocation (but not the wages) of individual employees on grounds of merit. We do not believe that either should have any place in profit sharing. Using a scheme in such a way would cause individual resentment and a general sense of unfairness, and would be a clear indication that profit sharing was incompatible with the management style of the company. Such conditions would also probably make a share-based scheme ineligible for Inland Revenue approval.

Determining total bonus fund

A very important question is how the total bonus is determined. There are those

---

Profit Sharing and Employee Shareholding Report, by D. Wallace Bell, Industrial Participation Association, 1980

who advocate that it should be on a discretionary basis, the board of directors deciding each year how much to allocate to profit sharing. We do not share their view. A discretionary bonus is apt to be regarded more as a paternalistic handout than as an equitable share of the profit, and can be a cause of dissatisfaction with employees feeling that it ought in fairness to be more. It is much better to have a fixed and known formula by which the total bonus fund and its division among the employees are calculated, so that everyone can see that they are receiving the proper amount.

The most appropriate formula for any company will depend on its own particular circumstances. There are however two principles which we believe should apply to any scheme. The first is that the formula should generate bonuses only if a minimum profit sufficient for the company's reinvestment needs has been attained – a profit threshold. The second is that the formula should be as simple as possible so that everyone can understand it.

In most firms a formula directly related to pre-tax profit will probably be suitable, e.g.:

- x% of profit (provided the threshold has been attained);
- x% of profit above the threshold;
- x% of increased profit over the previous year.

Some companies have a 'stepped' formula so that, in its simplest form, x becomes $x + y$ above a second threshold.

Other formulae are based on return on capital employed, return on sales, or the ratio of value added or turnover to payroll costs. And in some firms in specialized businesses an entirely different yardstick, possibly unique to the individual company, may be best. It is not for us in this book to examine all the various possibilities, but we would emphasize that there is no one 'best' formula, and any standard 'off the shelf' scheme is unlikely to be the best for most companies.*

Companies introducing profit sharing would also be well advised to do some calculations based on historical data over the past several years to see what would have been the result if a scheme with the proposed formula had been in operation over that period. Forward projections should be made as well, taking into account any anticipated changes in the future, and using minimum and maximum forecasts. It is not sufficient that the formula seems right for today; it must stand the test of time. Any scheme should however contain some provision for its periodical review. In a new scheme changes should not be made too soon, but no matter how carefully is has been designed not every detail will prove to be exactly right, so it should be looked at again after, say, three years. And as circumstances change there may need to be further reviews at later dates.

---

*Several profit sharing scheme formulae are examined in more detail in *Industrial Participation* by D. Wallace Bell, Pitman, 1979

It is also important to try to get the timing right when introducing a new scheme. If it is known that there will be major changes in the company in the next two or three years that will substantially affect the scheme, it is not the right time to start. There should be some confidence that the scheme will produce bonuses in the first years. Management cannot control the future and things may go wrong, but it will not generate much enthusiasm, nor management gain much credibility, if a profit sharing scheme is introduced with a great flourish in a year of record profit, and in the following year it pays out nothing. And a share-based scheme is not likely to increase loyalty if the first appropriation is made when the share price is at its all time high and all it does afterwards is go down.

All these considerations are important for the potential success of a profit sharing scheme, and its long-term effect. Many managements have found it helpful to visit other profit sharing companies of similar size, structure and type of workforce, to learn from their experience before finalizing their own scheme; and most profit sharing companies are very willing to share their experience in this way.*

Many managements considering the introduction of profit sharing use the services of a consultant at some stage in the process. This may sometimes be worthwhile, particularly in preparing the formal documentation for schemes requiring Inland Revenue approval, but there can be pitfalls. It may be in the interest of the consultant to encourage management to proceed with the introduction of a scheme even if the company is actually not ready for it; or to suggest some entirely different form of financial participation which is not what management really wants. It may also be in his interest to recommend an 'off the shelf' scheme with only minor modifications, rather than one which is tailored throughout to meet the needs of the company. At the end of the day top management has to be completely satisfied that what is proposed is indeed right for its company. It is they who will have to live with the consequences of whatever scheme is adopted.

The next stage, having decided on the essential elements of the scheme, is the preparation for its introduction. There will be some technical matters – drawing up the rules of the scheme, and if it is to be an approved share-based scheme, submitting them to the Inland Revenue. Shareholders' authorization may also be required for the issue of new shares.

Communication with employees

The most important task will be communication with the employees. First, there should be discussions with the management team. These should have begun long before the details were finalized, so that managers are kept fully in the picture. The next task is informing the trade union or other employee representatives, and the

---

*The Industrial Participation Association can assist in arranging such visits

workforce generally. Again, it would have been wise to inform them of the intention to introduce profit sharing, with a forecast of the likely timetable, once the decision had been taken to go ahead. Now will be the time to give them the details.

In most companies the basis for this is an explanatory booklet, usually in question and answer form. But the style of such booklets varies greatly, from the serious to the humorous with cartoons, so it would be worth getting a selection from different companies to examine the range and consider what might be most suitable. Many firms expand on the booklet in a video or tape-slide presentation used as the basis for discussion in small groups. This is most suitable when such presentations are a normal means of communication in the company, and is particularly useful in multi-site organizations.

Any verbal communication about the scheme, whether or not in relation to a visual presentation, should be by specialists able to answer all questions immediately. A profit sharing scheme, especially a share scheme, is not really suitable for communication through a briefing group system where many of the people doing the briefings may not fully understand it themselves. But the 'specialists' should be staff who are used to communicating in simple layman's language, not those who would be likely to explain things in terms understood only by accountants!

There will need also to be continuing communication about the scheme even after its introduction. New employees will have to be told about it, preferably as part of their induction course. If there is a qualifying period of service before employees can participate, most of those not in the scheme from the start will probably have forgotten what they were originally told about it by the time they do qualify, and should be given some form of refresher course. There is also the problem experienced by many profit sharing companies of how to keep up interest between the bonus payments – or does the effect wear off in two weeks? Interest is not likely to be maintained unless management provides regular reports on the company's progress, if possible with some indication of how the profit sharing bonus is building up compared with the previous year; and these reports can be the basis for stimulating discussion at all levels about ways in which performance could be improved.

It is through such means that profit sharing can be used to generate among employees an interest in the firm's performance that will encourage them to do what they can to contribute to its success. In introducing profit sharing, in the design of the scheme, and in its integration with other processes of employee participation in the company, one of management's aims should be to get as much mileage as possible from it.

Profit sharing in private companies

All the considerations relating to profit sharing in general apply equally to private as to public limited companies, but there are some additional points that should be taken into account by private firms in relation to share-based schemes. These are how the shares will be valued, and what will be the market for them when employees wish to sell their shares. If the company intends to go public within a relatively short time there is little difficulty because the employee shareholders can expect to see a substantial appreciation in the value of their shares on the flotation, and thereafter there will be an open market for them. If however the present owners intend to keep it as a private company for the foreseeable future, there can be problems.

The question of there being a market for the shares when employees come to sell them is not so great a problem as it used to be, because the company can now itself purchase them – provided, of course, it has the resources to do so. Some companies have also arranged an internal market among the employees themselves, and in a few cases an employee shareholding trust is a willing purchaser. It must be realized, however, that under an approved profit sharing scheme, employees leaving the company can remain shareholders at least up to the release date when their shares become free from any income tax liability on their disposal, although technically the shares are held by the trustees of the scheme until then. Before the Finance Act 1986 enabled companies to put a restriction on shares issued under a profit sharing scheme, requiring them to be disposed of when employees leave (or when they become free of any tax liability if the employee has left before then), there was the real possibility of small packets of shares being held indefinitely by ex-employees, or their heirs, with whom the company had long lost contact. That is no longer a problem provided the company does put such a restriction on the shares; and any private company with any form of employee share scheme would be well advised to do so.

Valuation of the shares poses a bigger problem, especially for small family businesses. Typically, a private company's shares are considerably undervalued compared with what they would be worth if they were quoted on the Stock Exchange. If the employees acquire shares in the company through a profit sharing scheme they will expect to see their shares appreciate as the company prospers, and provided the share valuation keeps pace with performance, in theory there should be no difficulty – the base price at which they acquire them should be irrelevant. In practice, however, it may not be so simple. The value attached to the shares of a private company is often based on a number of factors, and for various reasons the controlling shareholders may not wish it to be more directly related to profit. Unless therefore a private company is prepared to have a realistic valuation made of its shares, it may be better to have a cash rather than a share-based profit sharing scheme.

CHAPTER 8

What of the future?

Profit sharing in the UK has increased significantly over the past 10–15 years. When it has been introduced as part of an overall policy of developing employee involvement and participation it has generally had a positive impact on employee attitudes and encouraged the kind of cooperation and commitment that is necessary for any company to be successful. Profit sharing, and employee shareholding that is increasingly associated with it, is also now accepted as 'a good thing' by all the main political parties, by employers' organizations, and by a growing number of trade unionists.

If it is also good for the national economy – and the better performance of profit sharing companies compared with non-profit sharers as shown by our project suggests that it must be – it is to be hoped that the spread of profit sharing will continue and indeed accelerate, so that for industry and commerce as a whole it becomes the norm rather than the exception, as has already happened in some few sectors. It should be actively encouraged by government and all who are concerned with the well-being and future prosperity of UK Limited.

We sense, however, that attention is sometimes being diverted by other forms of financial participation, also encouraged by tax concessions, that may be attractive in themselves but are no substitute for all-employee profit sharing. There are four main types:

- contributory schemes;
- share option schemes;
- profit-related pay;
- share participation through privatization or flotations.

Contributory schemes

It is possible to use the tax concessions of the Finance Act 1978 for contributory share schemes in which the company offers each year to provide one free share (or more than one) for every share purchased by employees from their own resources. The company may determine the maximum amount of profit it is prepared to put into the scheme each year (for subscription for the free shares) and based on its anticipation of the probable take-up, the maximum level of individual participation. If applications are received in excess of expectations, they would be scaled down *pro rata* as necessary; if applications are below expectations, the company would actually put less money into the scheme than it had allocated to it.

The shares provided by the company are free of income tax and are held by trustees on exactly the same terms as in a conventional profit sharing scheme approved under the provisions of the Finance Act 1978. There are, however, no tax concessions attaching to the shares purchased by the employees, but they must also be held by trustees, for a period determined by the company – usually one or two years. They can then be 'recirculated' for another matching offer in a later year. The first, and by far the largest, scheme of this kind is in British Petroleum.

From the point of view of employees who want, or are willing, to invest in the company, it is very attractive. In the first allocation they effectively get shares at half-price or less; later on, if they recirculate the shares they originally purchased, they will get additional shares free of cost.

From the point of view of the company, it is encouraging share participation, but requiring a commitment on the part of the employees, by putting some of their own money into the scheme to purchase shares, as a condition for the company's matching contribution.

For employees, however, except for those who participate up to the maximum level permitted, it is clearly not profit sharing in any real sense. Their individual benefit from the scheme has no relation to the company's profitability. It is determined simply by the depth of their own pockets and what other demands there are on their financial resources.

Share option schemes

These are of two kinds: save-as-you-earn (SAYE) schemes approved under the provisions of the Finance Act 1980; and selective schemes approved under the terms of the Finance Act 1984.

SAYE share option schemes

To participate in these schemes, employees must contract to save, through a building society or national savings, a minimum of £10 to a maximum of £100 per month for a period of five years.* At the commencement of their contract they are given options over shares to the value of their total savings over the five years plus the predetermined bonus (equivalent to interest) added at the end of that period; the valuation of the shares being their market value at the start of the savings period, discounted by a maximum of 10%. At the end of the five years (or in some schemes,

---

*These are the present (1987) minimum and maximum participation levels. Originally they were lower; they may be raised again in the future

at the end of seven years with extra bonus added to their savings) they may either exercise the option in whole or in part, or let it lapse and withdraw their accumulated savings and bonus in cash. Employees' savings are therefore not at risk even if the share price has fallen below the option price.

The tax concessions are that there is no income tax on the bonus added to the employees' savings, and the only tax liability in the event of employees exercising their option and purchasing the shares is capital gains tax (if any) on their eventual sale.

To be approved the scheme must be open to all full-time UK employees who have completed five years' continuous service in the company, but as with profit sharing schemes, companies are free to include other employees if they wish, e.g. part-timers and those with a shorter period of service. But actual participation in the scheme is on a self-selection basis by the employees themselves, both whether to participate at all, and if so, at what level. (Management can however impose a lower maximum level of participation for all employees than the £100 per month currently allowed by the legislation.)

Up to March 1987, 618 SAYE share option schemes had been approved. In many companies these are in addition to approved profit sharing schemes, so although it is correct to say that in all, over 1200 all-employee share schemes have been introduced under the 1978 and 1980 Acts together, the number of companies operating schemes is much less.

Except for a few mainly high technology service companies in which the take-up rate for SAYE share option schemes has been over 50%, in most firms it is not much above 15%, and often much lower at shop-floor level in manufacturing and labour-intensive industries. Compared with profit sharing it is not, in our view, a very attractive scheme for most employees. Conceptually, it means coming to terms not only with what a share is, but with an option over a share. It requires a deliberate act of saving, and a commitment to save a fixed amount for five years, which is a deterrent to people on relatively low incomes, especially those with families to support.

In contrast to profit sharing, the employee who joins the scheme does not become a shareholder for at least five years, and the probability is that he will not become a long-term shareholder even then. If when his savings contract matures the share price is higher than the option price and he exercises the option, circumstances at that time may well lead him to sell the shares almost at once. He will be faced with an entirely different kind of decision from that when he joined the scheme. That decision was 'I can afford to save (say) £40 a month'. After five years, however, and assuming a rise in the share price of only 50% over the option price, the decision then will be 'Do I want to keep the shares and have £5000 invested in the company I work for – or should I treat it as a windfall and buy a new car?' or whatever may be his most pressing need or desire at that time.

The same kind of decision is less likely to arise under a profit sharing scheme when annual tranches of shares held by trustees are released, firstly because the sums involved will, for most employees, be of a different magnitude – a few hundred rather than a few thousand pounds; and secondly because the participant knows he has other tranches of shares in the pipeline that will follow later. There is always a tendency to stay with established and continuing processes, whereas watersheds more often result in a change of course.

SAYE share option schemes are not, therefore, in our view likely to lead to widespread or long-term employee shareholding, especially in firms that do not have a profit sharing scheme under the Finance Act 1978. In companies that do have such schemes, however, an SAYE scheme can provide a convenient way for those employees who wish to do so to 'top up' the shareholding they are building up through profit sharing.

It may also be the best that can be offered as an all-employee share scheme in a conglomerate in which a share-based profit sharing scheme would be inappropriate, but it should not be regarded as an adequate alternative to cash profit sharing schemes in its subsidiary companies.

Selective share option schemes

It has long been the practice in some companies to offer senior executives options over a specified number of shares to be exercised at some time in the future, usually between three and seven years from the date of the option. In a few companies, such options were offered to all employees in a scheme running in parallel with an SAYE share option scheme. There had been various proposals for special tax treatment for such schemes, but until 1984 any gain in value of the shares at the time the option was exercised was regarded as a benefit arising from employment and taxed as income. The Finance Act 1984, however, made provision for approved selective share option schemes in which there is no tax liability at the time the option is exercised, and only capital gains tax liability on any increase in value over the option price if and when the shares are sold.

Options may be granted only to full-time directors (defined as normally devoting at least 25 hours per week to the duties of the office) and employees contracted to work at least 20 hours per week. Subject to those limits the company is entirely free to decide who to include. The options may be over shares whose initial value is up to four times the individual's annual salary or £100 000, whichever is the greater. To attract the tax concessions they must be exercised between three and ten years after the option date, and if partially exercised, only once in any three year period.* The Investment Protection Committees currently limit the number of shares which may be put under option in this scheme to not more than 5% of the company's issued ordinary share capital over ten years (and not more than 10% of the share capital to all employee share schemes combined).

---

*These are the original conditions which have not so far (April 1987) been changed

By March 1987, 2959 discretionary share option schemes had already been submitted to the Inland Revenue for approval under the provisions of the 1984 Finance Act, and 2204 had so far been approved. And although a few companies grant options over a relatively small number of shares to a fairly large number of senior managers, most limit them to a small group of directors and very senior executives, in some cases to just one or two people.

Clearly these options are of very great potential benefit to the recipients. At no risk to themselves, and without even having to save in advance, the participants stand to make a substantial gain from any increase in the company's share price, for whatever reason, and they can time the exercise of their options to when they judge the price to be at its peak. They will have no difficulty in arranging a short-term bank loan to cover the purchase if they undertake immediately to sell sufficient shares to repay the loan, and thereafter they can if they wish take advantage of capital gains tax exemption limits by selling their remaining shares in yearly tranches.

The early proponents of tax concessions for selective share option schemes believed they would promote an entrepreneurial spirit among senior managers; but the true entrepreneur has his own fortune at risk – he stands to lose, as well as gain. In companies which attach strict performance achievement conditions to the exercise of the options there is perhaps some element of entrepreneurship, but most do not, and the consequence is that substantial share options are rapidly becoming a necessary condition for top executives to be willing to join, or remain with, most leading companies.

The 2204 selective share option schemes introduced in less than three years is in marked contrast to the 634 all-employee profit sharing schemes approved over nearly nine years since the 1978 Finance Act. This again suggests that the boards of directors of many British companies have so far failed to realise that real success depends on the commitment and cooperation of everyone in the enterprise, and that it is just as important to motivate those with the lowest incomes whose jobs are least likely to provide other, non-financial rewards, as it is to motivate and reward those at the top. Substantial share options limited to the top management group in companies that have no other profit sharing or share scheme involving employees generally certainly cannot be seen as contributing anything to employee participation.

Profit-related pay

The 1987 Finance Bill proposed tax concessions for profit-related pay which, possibly with some amendments, were intended to be included in the Finance Act.*

---

*Because of the dissolution of Parliament and the general election in June 1987 the proposals were not included in the shortened 1987 Finance Act, but they have been revived in a later Act. This description is based on the proposals as set out in the original 1987 Finance Bill

A profit-related pay (PRP) scheme may be introduced by any private sector employer, incorporated or unincorporated, whose business 'is carried on with a view to profit'; and it may apply to a group, a subsidiary, or a sub-unit of either, provided only that it can produce audited profits. Schemes must be registered with the Inland Revenue to benefit from the tax concessions, and they must last for at least one year.

A scheme must include at least 80% of all full-time employees (those contracted to work 20 hours or more per week) who have completed more than three years service, and they must participate on similar terms, e.g. proportionate to salary or length of service. These are minimum requirements; the scheme may include other employees as well, but controlling directors are excluded.

The 'distributable PRP pool' must be either a straight percentage of profits or a sum that varies in line with changes in annual profits. In the first year it must be such as would amount to at least 5% of the total pay, including the PRP, of all participating employees if profits are unchanged from the previous year. But there is a threshold and a ceiling. Scheme rules may provide that there would not be any distribution if profits are below an amount which would produce a PRP pool of 5% of pay, and profits in excess of 160% of the previous year's may be disregarded.

The tax relief applies to the PRP received by individual employees, i.e. their share of whatever the PRP pool (if any) turns out to be. But there is a limit to the amount of PRP to which the tax relief will apply: 20% of total pay including the PRP, or £3000, whichever is the lower. Up to these limits, half the PRP will be free from income tax. (This does not, however, limit the amount of PRP employees may actually receive; only the amount eligible for tax relief.)

Payments of PRP may be made annually or more frequently; but as the actual PRP pool cannot be known before the end of the 'profit period', defined as 12 months, tax relief on interim payments would be subject to adjustment after the accounts are audited – there will be no tax relief on any payments made in excess of the total PRP pool for the year.

Profit-related pay is clearly intended to constitute part of basic pay, and in our view has more to do with pay flexibility than with profit sharing. Certainly if profits increase, employees should get something in addition to their current pay; if profits are unchanged, their pay should remain the same (and they would benefit from the tax relief on the PRP element in it); but if profits fall, they stand to lose part of their basic pay, and the tax relief will not make up for that.

The provision that there need not be any PRP distribution if profits fall below a level which would produce a pool of 5% of pay, taken in conjunction with the stipulation that in the first year the formula must produce a minimum of 5% if profits remain unchanged, are in our view indicative of the thinking behind the proposals. If in the first year profits fall (by however little), schemes which incorporate the threshold provision need not make any PRP payout at all, and employees' pay would automatically fall by 5% or whatever higher proportion had been determined as constituting the PRP element in their total pay, and the same could apply in subsequent years.

The PRP element could of course be instead of a pay increase, provided it was 5% or more, so that current earnings were protected, and the risk was limited to the increment. Even so, employees are likely to regard as 'theirs' – as their basic pay – the total amount including the increase.

Companies which already have cash profit sharing schemes in which the bonuses are usually more than 5% of pay may wish to consider registering them as PRP schemes in order to give their employees the benefit of the tax concessions. The PRP proposals are, however, not primarily aimed at companies that already have profit sharing, but at those that do not.

We have discussed in Chapter 1 the likely effect on employee attitudes of PRP compared with profit sharing, and in our view mainstream, proven forms of profit sharing which do not put any part of basic pay at risk are greatly superior to these proposals for profit-related pay. Any company which is ready for profit sharing would do much better to introduce a conventional type of scheme, if possible associated with employee shareholding by being approved under the provisions of the 1978 Finance Act. This is also much more tax-efficient than PRP as not only is there no income tax payable on the whole of the bonus, but no National Insurance contributions by either employer or employee. And even those organizations which are not able to have share schemes would in our view do better to have cash profit sharing rather than PRP. It is not worth forfeiting the real long-term benefits of profit sharing in order to gain a little tax relief. But companies which are not ready for profit sharing are not likely to derive any real benefit from PRP, and should not introduce it just because it offers tax concessions.

Share participation through privatization or flotations

In the privatization of state-owned enterprises such as British Telecom and British Gas, in which shares are offered to the public, and in the flotation of a major 'public' institution such as the Trustee Savings Bank, it has become common practice to encourage widespread employee shareholding by giving, or offering, shares to employees on special terms. One or more of three methods are used.

(a) All employees (or all with a relatively short qualifying period of service) may be given a small number of free shares, usually to a value of under £100. These are issued under the provisions of the Finance Act 1978 and held by trustees on the same terms as in an approved profit sharing scheme.

(b) Employees may be offered a rather higher, but still relatively small, number of free 'matching' shares provided they themselves subscribe, and pay, for an equal number. This is exactly the same as in the contributory schemes described earlier; the matching shares are issued under the 1978 Finance Act provisions, and both lots of shares are held by trustees.

(c) Employees may be given preference over the general public in the allocation of shares if the issue is oversubscribed, by applying on special 'pink forms'. (This is common practice in most flotations, and is not peculiar to privatizations.)

In the privatization of Rolls Royce (May 1987), as well as a small allocation of free shares, employees were offered two matching shares for each one bought up to a value of £150, a 10% discount on further shares purchased up to a value of £2000, and priority allocation up to a further £10 000 worth of shares.

The privatization of very large organizations such as British Telecom and British Gas has led to a spectacular increase in the number of employee shareholders, and as the shares issued under (a) and (b), which account for the great majority, cannot be sold for two years, they will remain shareholders for at least that period and probably longer. This has been seized on by the advocates of wider share ownership generally, and partially accounts for the increased number of individual UK shareholders over the past few years. Realistically, however, it is not very significant for an individual to hold only £100 or so of shares in just one company; and shareholding at that level, if there is no more to come, is not likely to have any influence on employee attitudes. In a typical share-based profit sharing scheme, with bonuses of say 5% of annual salary, in five years an employee on average earnings would accumulate shares to the value of about £2500.

Companies offering small numbers of shares to employees on their flotation should follow up their original offer with a fully fledged profit sharing scheme – only then can they hope to see any real benefit from employee shareholding. We are pleased to note that some have now done so.

Employees as shareholders

When employees become shareholders in the company they work for, there is an important change in their status. They become members in the full sense, able to vote for (or against!) the re-election of directors, and on all the other matters which under company law must be put to the shareholders. They also stand to share in the company's success through dividend payments and an increasing share price – and they stand to lose if it is not successful.

In the long term, if employee shareholding were to increase significantly it could also have an impact on management's accountability for the way it runs the business. Whereas at present directors are generally accountable to many external, often impersonal and institutional, shareholders with little interest in the company except in deciding whether to hold or sell its shares, they could come to realise that they are increasingly accountable to many employee shareholders who know a great deal about how the company is doing, and could be very critical if they see things are going wrong – or supportive if they are going well.

Institutional investors have been said in the past not to favour employee shareholders because they might use their influence to further their own short-term interests as employees, rather than act in the long-term interests of the shareholders generally. In reality, however, it is often the institutional investors who take a short-term view as portfolio performance becomes all important, and it is employee shareholders who are most concerned with a company's long-term prosperity, and who are in a much better position than outside shareholders to monitor its progress.

We believe therefore that while the Investment Protection Committees are right in limiting the number of shares that may be put under option in a selective share option scheme, they are wrong in putting such a stringent limit on the remaining shares available for all-employee schemes. Certainly individual outside shareholders, who are usually much more loyal to a company, and more concerned with its long-term performance, than institutional investors, have nothing to fear, and much to gain from all-employee shareholding through profit sharing increasing to 10% or more in their company.

The future

What, then, of the future? If Britain is to re-establish a leading position in the world economy – or even to avoid slipping still further down the scale – we will have to find some way of generating a commitment to success at every level of our industrial and commercial activity. But that can only be done in each individual enterprise, by its own management positively involving all employees in a common and willing effort to improve performance. And in securing and maintaining that commitment in the private sector profit sharing, linked where possible to employee shareholding, is one of the most effective means available.

The future of profit sharing, and indeed the future of the British economy, will be determined by the policies and practices that British managers establish in their own companies. But business operates within a framework that is largely created by government. That framework should in our view be positively and consistently supportive of mainstream, proven forms of all-employee profit sharing that, as the experience of so many companies has shown, can contribute to success. It will not encourage the extension of profit sharing if management's attention is constantly being diverted to other forms of participation by changing tax incentives. But the framework should be supportive, not compulsive. Profit sharing should never be imposed in the UK by legislation. It should result from action taken in individual companies by their own managements, and not just because of tax concessions, but because they see it as essentially right – right for their employees, and right for their companies. And if there is a macro-economic objective in profit sharing it is that it might move the UK towards a high-performance, high-reward economy based on high-performance, high-reward organizations that are the mark of our most successful international competitors. We might even be encouraged to move in that direction by the much wider experience of profit sharing in some other countries that is reviewed in the next chapter.

CHAPTER 9

Profit sharing in the USA, France and Japan

United States of America

As in the UK, profit sharing in the USA has a long history. It is claimed that the first plan was established by Albert Gallatin, Secretary of the Treasury under Jefferson and Madison, at his glass works in New Geneva, Pennsylvania, in 1797. Progress in the nineteenth century was slow, but Colonel William Cooper Procter set up the Procter and Gamble plan in 1887 and this is probably the earliest plan which has continued up to the present day.* The idea began to spread in the twentieth century and some of the most famous plans were established between 1910 and 1920: Eastman Kodak, Sears Roebuck, Harris Trust & Savings Bank, and Johnson Wax. After the relative inactivity of the depression years, new interest in profit sharing was created by a penetrating study by the Senate Finance Committee in 1939 which stated that:

'The committee finds that profit sharing in one form or another has been and can be eminently successful, when properly established, in creating employer–employee relations that make for peace, equity, efficiency, and contentment. We believe it to be essential to the ultimate maintenance of the capitalistic system'.

Following these favourable findings Congress quickly passed legislation which provided tax advantages for companies and their employees in the case of deferred profit sharing plans which met certain conditions. This had two consequences. First, it led to a positive explosion of interest in this kind of profit sharing, so that the number of plans rose from zero in 1939 to 375 000 in 1984. Second, it changed the nature of profit sharing in the US so that a prime motive for introducing it became the provision of a retirement income or benefits in the event of disability, death or the termination of employment before retirement. However, 'traditional' cash profit sharing, which has no tax concessions, has also continued to thrive. Today it seems that there are altogether about 500 000 profit sharing plans in the

*American terminology refers to profit sharing 'plans' whereas in the UK we more commonly use 'schemes'

USA covering a total of some 20 million employees. The deferred plans alone cover about one-fifth of private, non-farm employment. They exist in approximately one out of every four manufacturing companies; one out of three retailers and wholesalers; and in about 40% of banks. The nature of this astonishing growth and the way in which it has taken place will now be considered in more detail.

Cash profit sharing

This is the traditional form of profit sharing in the USA. The bonus, which is linked to the profitability of the company, is normally paid once or twice a year and its annual value might be equivalent to about six weeks' pay. Cash plans have been introduced by small (fewer than 25 employees) to large (more than 250 000 employees) companies in almost every sector of the private economy. Such plans require no official approval, and there are no official records of them, but in 1974 the Profit Sharing Research Foundation estimated their number at about 100 000. Since then, profit sharing has become more popular, not less.

As in the UK, although the principle is the same the precise nature of profit sharing will vary from one company to another. Johnson Wax is a US-based multinational company which introduced cash profit sharing in 1917 and added a deferred plan in 1953. Among the special features of cash profit sharing in this company are first, that it applies to most overseas as well as US employees; and second, that profit shares are based on locally earned profits. So in 1982 most US employees of the company received a cash bonus equivalent to about six weeks' pay, while in a very few of the most profitable overseas companies long-service employees received as much as 20 weeks' basic pay.

Deferred profit sharing

Whereas cash profit sharing has developed in the USA without tax concessions, deferred profit sharing, its younger but now much bigger brother, has been dependent on tax concessions since birth. In fact some commentators have described it as the 'common man's tax shelter'. Under existing US tax law, payments up to 15% of employee remuneration made by an employer to a profit sharing trust for the benefit of employees qualify as deductible business expenses. The employee also pays no tax on the employer's payments or on the income earned from their investment, and is taxed only at capital gains tax rates when the final distribution is made, normally at retirement. These schemes have to be approved by the Inland Revenue Service and consequently quite accurate statistics are available for the number of schemes approved, terminated and continuing. Table 9.1 shows the way in which these schemes have spread at an incredible rate since the provision of tax concessions in 1939.

Table 9.1 *Number of qualified deferred profit sharing plans in the USA 1939–1984 (approvals minus terminations)*

Year	Number of Plans (Cumulative Total)
1939	37
1949	3 565
1959	20 204
1969	87 219
1979	261 261
1984	374 557

Source: Profit Sharing Research Foundation calculations based on US Treasury Department reports.

Most of these plans cover a small number of participants and were introduced in small companies which sometimes lack the financial resources to afford pensions with rigid contributions and indeterminable future costs. For example, over the 20-year period 1965–1984 the total number of schemes approved was 400 000 and the total number of participants in these schemes was 10 900 000 (though some of these were subsequently terminated). Thus the average number of participants per plan was 27 when the plan was introduced. But to emphasize the small size of most deferred profit sharing companies is not to suggest that the plans are therefore unimportant. A 1984 survey showed that of 234 companies with fewer than 100 participants in a deferred plan 181, or 77%, had no pension plan. Consequently, the deferred profit sharing plan was the principal means by which these companies provided for the retirement security of their employees. And that is true for many other similar companies. Statistics compiled by the Profit Sharing Research Foundation showed that in 1984 capital assets invested in securities through deferred profit sharing plans amounted to over $175 billion.

While it is generally accepted that retirement security is the primary goal of most deferred profit sharing plans, advocates of profit sharing insist that these plans also generate employee commitment to and involvement in the business. This helps to make the business more profitable and the benefits affordable. Thus the popularity of deferred profit sharing stems from its ability to achieve the twin aims of providing employees with retirement security and an incentive to work productively as a team.

The essential difference between a defined benefit pension plan and a deferred benefit profit sharing plan is that the former provides employees with a predetermined pension, funded on the basis of actuarial calculations. By contrast deferred profit sharing provides participants with an individual investment account arising out of contributions from the employer (and in about 60% of cases from employees, compulsorily or voluntarily). These contributions are invested in diversified securities by trustees and the value of the benefits will depend to some extent on the performance of the investments. The benefits are normally paid to participants in the form of a lump sum at the time of retirement.

Both pension and profit sharing plans have been affected by five major pieces of legislation since 1974: the Employee Retirement Income Security Act of 1974 (ERISA) triggered the most sweeping overhaul of pension and profit sharing plans in history; the Economic Recovery Tax Act of 1981 (ERTA) provided new opportunities for employees to make tax deductible contributions to a profit sharing trust; and the Tax Equity and Fiscal Responsibility Act of 1982 (TEFRA) together with the Tax Reform and the Retirement Equity Acts of 1984 made further changes in the law which required the amendment of most profit sharing plans. But the basic principle remains – that approved profit sharing plans designed to provide retirement security for employees attract substantial tax concessions, and that without these concessions most, if not all, deferred profit sharing plans would come to an end.

Finally, something must be said about employee stock ownership plans which have existed for many years but have received a new lease of life recently because of the tax benefits contained in ERISA and subsequent legislation. Most of the older plans, such as those at IBM, Sears Roebuck and Texas Instruments, provide for employee purchases of stock of the employing company, often at a discount or with matching funds provided by the employer. The newer plans, known as ESOPs, attract tax benefits and involve an outright contribution by an employer to an employee trust. Proponents of ESOPs claim that they provide an inexpensive way for a company to raise new capital or create a market for the shares of an owner while providing employees with a stake in the company's equity. They work as follows. A company sets up a special trust and contributes to it either its own stock (newly issued), cash to buy stock or cash to repay a loan which the trust takes out for the purpose of buying stock. Within limits these contributions are all tax deductible. The stock in the trust is allocated to employee accounts, usually on the basis of relative pay; generally all full-time employees with one year of service or more must benefit from the plan, receiving annual allocations over a period usually up to ten years. While the stock is in the trust the beneficiaries pay no tax on it and they pay only a minimal amount of tax when it is eventually distributed, usually, as in deferred profit sharing plans, on retirement.

The post-1974 tax benefits have led to a rapid expansion of ESOPs. In 1986 it was estimated that about 7500 ESOPs and stock bonus plans covered approximately 7.5 million workers.* For some ESOP advocates, stock ownership is the main goal. Others argue that it should be seen simply as one component in an overall programme of employee participation, in which profit sharing may also play a part. There are several similarities between ESOPs and deferred profit sharing plans. In particular, both kinds of plan are dependent on tax concessions. However, a major difference is that in an ESOP the fortunes of the beneficiaries are linked

---

*By the National Center for Employee Ownership. See *Employee Ownership*, May/June 1986, p.3

entirely to their own company's share price, while the assets of a deferred profit sharing plan are usually diversified, although 10% or more may be invested in the company's stock if the plan specifically authorizes such investment. Thus, if an ESOP company runs into financial difficulties the consequences can be catastrophic for the employees. Clearly, employees who are mainly concerned with retirement security will much prefer a deferred profit sharing plan or a defined pension plan to an ESOP.

Furthermore, as ESOPs are funded by a transfer of capital to the trust in no way related to the company's profit, they cannot really be regarded as profit sharing in any normal understanding of that concept. Apart from the tax benefits to the company, they are simply a means of making employees into shareholders. In contrast, the two forms of true profit sharing in the USA – cash plans and deferred plans – contain no element of individual employee shareholding.

France*

Although the first French experiments in profit sharing date back to the middle of the last century, the schemes that were introduced up until the 1960s remained limited to a few companies, being regarded with reservation or even hostility by most employers and trade unionists.

In the face of the widespread reluctance of both companies and trade unions, it was the public authorities which took the initiative through legislative measures in the cause of what was at the outset a political concept of profit sharing, the originator of which was General de Gaulle. His aim was the progressive improvement of the conditions of employees, which were still strongly marked by inequalities between the various parties.

Profit sharing in France is therefore part of a larger framework of participation which also includes, under financial participation, sharing in the capital as well as employee savings schemes provided by their companies.

The first significant statute was the law of 7 January 1959, which established optional profit sharing by which employees participate in their company's trading profits or improvements in its productivity. Under this statute companies were able to distribute to their employees, in addition to earnings, amounts exempt from taxes and social security charges, and these amounts were also deductible from the companies' taxable profits.

This statute did not have the impact hoped for, and this led the authorities to consider the introduction of stronger compulsory measures. Following the recommendations of a study commission, on 17 August 1967 the government adopted a statute which recognized that employees had a definite right to part of

*This report was prepared by J Remus, of FONDACT, and translated from the original in French

the profits of their employer. Its provisions were compulsory for all companies with over 100 employees, but could also be adopted voluntarily by firms with a smaller workforce.

A second statute passed on the same day – which emphasizes the connection seen in the mind of the legislature between the two laws – established savings schemes specifically for companies, intended to collect the voluntary savings of employees.

Since 1967 there has been a succession of other statutes mainly dealing with employee shareholding – with share options by a law of 31 December 1970, with shareholding schemes by a law of 27 December 1973, and with the free distribution of shares by a law of 24 October 1980, this on the initiative of the President of the Republic, M. Giscard d'Estaing.

Under the socialist administration the range was extended even further, with the establishment of wage-earner funds (*fonds salariaux*) and the adoption of mechanisms for buying out companies inspired by the methods of the leveraged management buy-outs much practised in the USA and the UK. Although the wage-earner funds have not survived the electoral defeat of the socialists in 1986, the buying out of companies by employees is becoming more and more accepted in France. One can expect new developments in the coming years, as gradually the retirement of company leaders in ever larger numbers begins to highlight the question of the perpetuity of companies and in consequence of their succession.

By the beginning of 1986, France possessed a large body of legal texts dealing with financial participation of employees in their companies. They had been drawn up over the years, one after the other, and proved to be complicated, poorly coordinated and characterized by many regulations which deterred companies from bringing the schemes into effect.

The government which emerged from the elections of 16 March 1986, having stood as heir to the Gaullist tradition, was committed to promoting profit sharing, but adapted it to the new economic circumstances and strove to give more homogeneity to the mass of legal texts. Hence the law of 21 October 1986 which, without disrupting the existing framework, was intended to make it more coherent, to remove the administrative approval procedures and to increase the tax advantages. This statute includes three chapters dealing with two different forms of profit sharing (deferred and immediate), and with company savings schemes.

In putting the accent on profit sharing in this description of financial participation in France, savings schemes are not dealt with, except to emphasize that they may receive, apart from the voluntary contributions of the employees, which are generally deducted from their pay, amounts arising from profit sharing, either from compulsory schemes under the provisions of the earlier legislation, or from new schemes under the statute of 21 October 1986.

Deferred profit sharing *(La participation aux resultats)*

The compulsory profit sharing under the 1967 statute constitutes the most original aspect of the French system of financial participation, and was not changed substantially by the statute of 21 October 1986. All companies with 100 employees or more are obliged to reserve a part of their profits for their employees, determined by a formula that has not been changed since 1967. The profit for this purpose is defined as one half of the taxable profit after deducting a remuneration on capital employed of 5%. The proportion attributed to the employees is based on this amount multiplied by the ratio of total payroll to value added; a formula intended to reflect the proportionate contribution made by the labour force to profit. This constitutes a floor, but participation agreements may provide for different bases and methods of calculation, so long as they result, from the same taxable or accounting profit, in at least equivalent benefits for the employees.

The profit sharing established by this law has the following features.

1. It constitutes a right of the employees, but the allocation any individual may receive is subject to two limits:

(i) the salary taken into consideration to determine the share of each employee must not exceed four times the maximum salary which is subject to social security contributions, currently about 110 000 francs per year;

(ii) the actual share per employee must not exceed half of the maximum salary as so determined.

2. It is tied to a requirement to save, and as a result the company's accounts include a 'profit sharing special reserve' and employees cannot withdraw their own profit share from it until after the end of a five-year period (apart from exceptional cases where earlier release is permitted). The law of 21 October 1986 enables the release period to be shortened to three years; but the tax exemption on the amount received by the employee, which is total if the funds are blocked for the five-year period, is then reduced to one half.

3. Profit sharing benefits from a privileged tax arrangement which applies equally to the employer as to the employee. The company does not have to pay either social security charges or tax on the amounts allocated to employees under the scheme, and it can deduct the total amount of the profit sharing when calculating the tax payable on its own profits. It can also make a tax-deductible provision on investments up to 30% of any amount put into the profit sharing special reserve in excess of the minimum laid down by the statute.

4. Profit sharing is the subject of an agreement between the employer and the representatives of the employees, most frequently the company committees, and the

agreement thus negotiated specifies the methods by which the employees are kept informed, and the ways in which the profit sharing funds are held or invested. These may include:

(i) the allocation of the company's own shares; these shares may result from the incorporation of reserves into capital, or from a prior purchase made by the company;

(ii) the allocation of sums of money to a fund which the employer has to devote to investment; the employees acquiring a claim on the company in the form of blocked current accounts;

(iii) the acquisition of shares in mutual funds governed by provisions specially drawn up by the companies and their employees;

(iv) the allocation of amounts into company savings schemes in which the payments from profit sharing join those coming from voluntary deductions from earnings or from other profit sharing schemes.

By 31 December 1985, 10 336 profit sharing agreements had been signed of which 7 104 were under statute and 3 153 were outside its provisions. The number of companies involved was 11 965, the number of employees working in these companies was 4 550 000, and the number of actual beneficiaries (at the end of December 1983) was 2 592 000.

The global total of the profit sharing special reserves released during the financial year 1983 (the last year for which figures are available) was 6 050 billion francs; the amount of profit share per employee was 2 335 francs, that is about 3% of average earnings.

It is interesting to note that direct allocation of the company's shares has rarely been the chosen method (0.37%); the main method of allocation of profit sharing was in blocked current accounts (56.83%), or as parts of mutual funds, whether or not within the scope of savings schemes.

Introduced under the compulsory provisions of statutory law, deferred profit sharing has been sufficiently extensively adopted. It does not seem likely that there will be substantial new developments because it already covers all the companies that are subject to it by reason of their number of employees and of their profit-making capacity. The movement's further expansion depends on the achievement of greater profits by French companies.

Immediate profit sharing *(L'interessement des salariés)*

Under the statute of 7 January 1959 profit sharing involved an immediate distribution of funds to the employees. Little practised until recently, immediate profit sharing has been the subject of renewed interest during the past few years when restrictions on general increases of salaries have encouraged companies to seek other forms of remuneration related to their financial health.

Aware of the attractions that immediate profit sharing offers in present circumstances, the legislature of 1986 undertook to make it still more appealing to companies. It removed the long and often discouraging approval procedures and replaced them by a simple deposit of a form with the Department of Labour; and provided that the amounts distributed could be as much as 20% of gross payroll, which is considerable. Profit sharing could also henceforth be limited to categories of employees and/or based on work units, which enables it to be designed in accordance with the social or geographical characteristics of the enterprise.

This form of profit sharing, as well as being voluntary, has the following characteristics.

1. As with deferred profit sharing, it is based on an agreement negotiated with representatives of the employees. The agreement is for a period of three years, and it must include arrangements for keeping the staff informed.

2. On the other hand it does not embody a pre-established formula; the law requires only that it is linked to the trading results or to the increase in productivity or to any other form of collective remuneration that can form the basis for employee profit sharing.

3. There is no limit to the amount that any individual may receive, subject only to the global ceiling of 20% of gross payroll being observed.

4. The profit sharing funds are in principle immediately distributed to the beneficiaries, but are subject to income tax. If however the company has a savings scheme, the employee may allocate his profit share, up to an amount representing one half of his maximum earnings that are subject to social security deductions, into the savings scheme, and he will then pay no tax on this amount provided that it is held in the scheme for five years.

The possibility of supplying the savings scheme out of deferred profit sharing is in this way extended to immediate cash schemes. This emphasizes the intention to build bridges between the different systems of financial participation, so as to enable employees to build up some capital for themselves by various means.

At the end of 1985 the number of immediate profit sharing agreements had risen to 1180; 365 000 employees were involved. These figures may seem modest, but they represent a notable increase compared with the years 1978–80.

It is still too soon to measure the impact of the legislation stemming from the statute of 21 October 1986. It is however reasonable to expect, in the new economic context, a substantial development of immediate profit sharing schemes based on trading results or on the improvement of productivity.

Conclusion

As was emphasized at the beginning of this report, the various forms of profit sharing in France are closely interwoven. Thus company savings schemes may be resourced at the same time by the voluntary payments of the employees and by company contributions in the form of deferred or immediate profit sharing.

Similarly the funds may be used to invest in the company, in the form of shares, debentures or blocked accounts, or they may be diversified outside the company.

Although the amounts invested directly in company shares as a result of profit sharing are quite small, employee shareholding has nevertheless been given a considerable boost as a result of share option schemes and through savings schemes invested wholly or partially in the company's shares, with substantial inducements being offered for this type of investment.

It is to be noted also that employees in companies that are being privatized are being offered shares on very favourable terms, with a discount perhaps as high as 20% and the possibility of paying by instalments over two years.

Although compulsory profit sharing, which is the most original feature of the French system, is marking time, the whole range of voluntary forms of financial participation is today arousing a lively interest. For long regarded as gimmicks without any real economic significance, these forms may in the future be integrated into company policies, and financial participation may make good the inadequacies or expand the boundaries of traditional remuneration systems.

Japan*

Japan is sometimes held out as a prime example of profit sharing, but the twice-yearly bonus received by many Japanese employees has little relation to profit sharing as it is understood in the West, and is not regarded as such in Japan itself.

Its origins lie in the Japanese industrial system whereby in the 'large' companies, permanent full-time employees are exclusively recruited from school or college and have lifetime employment in the same firm until retirement. But retirement was, and still is in most companies, compulsory at the age of 55, while the rather meagre state pension was not payable until 65 (now reduced to 60). There was therefore a ten-year gap when retired employees had no income other than from their savings, at best supplemented by very much lower wages from part-time employment usually in the 'small' company sector. Company pensions payable on retirement were started only in the late 1960s and are still by no means universal. So in order to maintain smooth relations with employees during their lifetime employment, and avoid anxiety and discontent as it drew to a close, it became management policy in the large companies to provide a bonus which employees were, and still are, strongly encouraged to save so as to meet their needs in retirement.

While management may originally have regarded this as a bonus provided from

---

*This report is based on discussions with Japanese government, employers and trade union organizations, academics, and management and union representatives in many Japanese companies, during two visits to that country in 1981 and 1985

the company's profit, it has long since become a part of the total remuneration package negotiated annually with the unions in the 'shunto' or 'spring struggle', and once determined, is fixed until the next round of negotiations in the following year. It is defined as so many months' pay, normally varying, from company to company, between two and six months (i.e. a bonus of one to three months' pay in the summer, and a similar amount in the winter). In any individual company it varies little if at all from one year to another, although if profits have been particularly badly hit management may try to negotiate it down in the following year from, say, five months' pay to four, or if the company has become much more profitable, the union may try to negotiate it upwards.

For employees in receipt of bonus, therefore, it forms part of their negotiated, and assured, total annual income, but instead of receiving this in 12 equal monthly instalments, anything from a seventh to a third of the annual total is received in two extra instalments in June and December. In this it is comparable with the system in some European countries where one or even two extra months' wages are paid during the year.

Because the bonuses are primarily intended to be saved for retirement, many firms offer inducements to their employees to invest them in the company's own shares, adding a bonus of 5% or more to the employees' own investments. Employees thus become shareholders; but because of the share structure of Japanese companies, total employee shareholding in any company is usually below 1%. Nevertheless it is as a result of bonuses being invested in this or other ways that the Japanese are reputed to save a higher proportion of their total income than any other nation.

The actual amount of bonus which any individual receives depends primarily on pay, which includes seniority wage and an award for personal performance. But it may be reduced by absences. Bonus is not normally paid in respect of any days when the employee is absent for whatever reason except annual leave entitlement. (In many companies wages are not paid for absences either, which is why so many Japanese employees use some of their annual leave rather than be recorded as off sick.)

Another feature of the bonus is that it normally applies only to full-time permanent employees in the large company sector, and they constitute only 25% of the total workforce. There are some firms in the small company sector which do provide bonus, but they are the exceptions. And in some large firms, 50% or more of their own employees may be temporary or part-timers, not in the union, and not receiving bonus.

Profit sharing in Japan, therefore, as so many other things in that most intriguing country, is well designed to meet its own particular needs, but is by no means what, from outside, it may at first sight appear to be. But there is one similarity with profit sharing in the UK. Despite the bonus being part of the established annual wage, by being paid in a lump sum twice yearly it does not form part of the employees' regular monthly spendable income. Hence it can be saved for retirement without affecting the employees' standard of living; just as profit sharing bonuses in the UK which are over and above established *wages* or salaries – and the additional one or two months' wages in some other countries – can be used for special purposes which could not be met from regular spendable income.

APPENDICES

Profit sharing and non-profit sharing companies compared: sector results

Introduction

As explained in Chapter 4 our project was originally based on ten industrial and commercial sectors, but because in three of these sectors there were eventually too few of either profit sharing or non-profit sharing companies for valid comparison, the number was reduced to seven, the companies in the discarded sectors being included with 'miscellaneous'.

The seven sectors analysed separately are:

1. Building, timber, roads   (page 104)
2. Chemicals, plastics   (page 106)
3. Drapery and stores   (page 108)
4. Electricals   (page 110)
5. Engineering   (page 112)
6. Foods, groceries etc.   (page 114)
7. Miscellaneous (including beers, wines and spirits;
   industrials-miscellaneous; paper, printing, advertising; textiles) (page 116)

For each sector, the analysis was made for all nine ratios as for the composite results reported in Chapter 5, but so as not to overburden the reader with too many statistics, only six are included in the sector results:

1. Profitability ratios:

   (a) Return on capital employed
   (b) Earnings per share
   (c) Return on sales

2. Growth ratio:
   Growth in sales
3. Investor returns ratios:
   (a) Dividends per share
   (b) Total annual returns

The ratios omitted are:

- Return on equity: as noted in the composite results, this is usually roughly parallel with, but at a higher level than, return on capital employed;
- Growth in equity;
- Growth in profit: growth in sales, which we include, is, we feel, a more accurate measure of dynamic growth.

We have also omitted cumulative growth (which the reader can work out from the annual growth tables) and comparative ranking in the two top percentiles, which with relatively small numbers of companies in some sectors might not give a representative picture.

With the smaller number of companies in the sectors also, any individual aberrant result (an 'outlier') will have much more effect on the sector average, than in the composite results. For example, if out of a group of 100 companies one made an exceptional profit, or loss, in a particular year that resulted in its return on capital employed being $\pm$ 100%, whereas the average for the other 99 was 20%, it would alter the group average to 20.8% (if a profit) or 18.8% (if a loss). But if this outlier were one of a group of only ten, the average for the other nine being 20%, it would alter the group average to 28% (if a profit) or 8% (if a loss).

None of the company ratios was aberrant to such a degree, but readers will understand that any exceptional statistic in these sector results may be because of one or two outliers. This in no way detracts from the reliability of the overall results. Any aberrant company result is usually limited to one year, so even in a small group it will make very little difference to the group average over eight years.

We do not comment on the individual sector results. Our comments on the composite results in Chapter 5 apply in general also to the sectors.

In Appendix 2 there is a list of the profit sharing companies included in the project, under sectors. In a few cases these may be different from the companies' present names if after the end of their 1984/85 financial year they have been involved in a takeover or merger.

We do not list the non-profit sharing companies, because it would be invidious to name any individual company in a group whose average economic performance is shown to be inferior to that of a different group. As we have indicated more than once, the performance of any one company cannot be judged from the group average, and some of the non-profit sharers included in our project far surpassed some of the profit sharers.

Sector 1. Building, timber, roads

Number of companies:

Profit sharing	10
Non-profit sharing	40
Total	50

% Return on capital employed

	1977/ 78	1978/ 79	1979/ 80	1980/ 81	1981/ 82	1982/ 83	1983/ 84	1984/ 85	Average 8 years
Profit sharing companies	21.4	26.5	16.5	16.7	18.3	18.6	16.9	15.1	18.8
Non-profit sharing companies	20.6	19.0	17.9	12.8	11.6	14.0	13.7	11.8	15.2
Difference: profit sharers above (below) non-profit sharers	0.8	7.5	(1.4)	3.9	6.7	4.6	3.2	3.3	3.6

Earnings per share (pence)

	1977/ 78	1978/ 79	1979/ 80	1980/ 81	1981/ 82	1982/ 83	1983/ 84	1984/ 85	Average 8 years
Profit sharing companies	19.5	25.2	24.0	23.6	26.8	28.1	28.9	25.3	25.2
Non-profit sharing companies	14.3	15.1	18.0	11.2	10.9	13.7	17.1	12.9	14.2
Difference: profit sharers above (below) non-profit sharers	5.2	10.1	6.0	12.4	15.9	14.4	11.8	12.4	11.0

% Return on sales

	1977/ 78	1978/ 79	1979/ 80	1980/ 81	1981/ 82	1982/ 83	1983/ 84	1984/ 85	Average 8 years
Profit sharing companies	8.1	9.1	7.8	8.2	8.6	8.5	8.0	7.4	8.2
Non-profit sharing companies	6.2	6.1	5.9	4.7	4.0	4.4	5.3	4.7	5.2
Difference: profit sharers above (below) non-profit sharers	1.9	3.0	1.9	3.5	4.6	4.1	2.7	2.7	3.0

% Growth in sales

	1977/ 78	1978/ 79	1979/ 80	1980/ 81	1981/ 82	1982/ 83	1983/ 84	1984/ 85	Average 8 years
Profit sharing companies	18.6	21.5	14.7	10.0	7.8	15.8	23.5	6.8	**14.8**
Non-profit sharing companies	23.1	24.4	17.0	5.2	17.0	21.6	14.1	10.2	**16.6**
Difference: profit sharers above (below) non-profit sharers	(4.5)	(2.9)	(2.3)	4.8	(9.2)	(5.8)	9.4	(3.4)	**(1.8)**

Dividends per share (pence)

	1977/ 78	1978/ 79	1979/ 80	1980/ 81	1981/ 82	1982/ 83	1983/ 84	1984/ 85	Average 8 years
Profit sharing companies	4.8	6.2	6.9	5.2	6.2	7.3	7.6	6.2	**6.3**
Non-profit sharing companies	4.0	5.1	5.6	4.3	4.7	5.1	5.7	5.8	**5.0**
Difference: profit sharers above (below) non-profit sharers	0.8	1.1	1.3	0.9	1.5	2.2	1.9	0.4	**1.3**

Total annual investor returns (%)

	1978	1979	1980	1981	1982	1983	1984	1985	Average 8 years
Profit sharing companies	12.2	2.7	29.2	46.1	46.4	17.4	16.2	20.8	**23.9**
Non-profit sharing companies	36.1	18.6	13.0	14.6	26.6	19.2	12.4	23.5	**20.5**
Difference: profit sharers above (below) non-profit sharers	(23.9)	(15.9)	16.2	31.5	19.8	(1.8)	3.8	(2.7)	**3.4**

Sector 2. Chemicals, plastics

Number of companies:

Profit sharing	6
Non-profit sharing	12
Total	18

% Return on capital employed

	1977/ 78	1978/ 79	1979/ 80	1980/ 81	1981/ 82	1982/ 83	1983/ 84	1984/ 85	Average 8 years
Profit sharing companies	31.6	32.7	21.4	17.2	18.9	19.9	24.7	17.4	23.0
Non-profit sharing companies	22.9	21.3	16.5	8.3	12.5	13.9	14.6	15.5	15.7
Difference: profit sharers above (below) non-profit sharers	8.7	11.4	4.9	8.9	6.4	6.0	10.1	1.9	7.3

Earnings per share (pence)

	1977/ 78	1978/ 79	1979/ 80	1980/ 81	1981/ 82	1982/ 83	1983/ 84	1984/ 85	Average 8 years
Profit sharing companies	19.6	23.8	13.6	12.6	10.6	18.5	28.0	23.0	18.7
Non-profit sharing companies	12.2	16.0	13.2	9.2	9.8	11.9	13.5	12.0	12.2
Difference: profit sharers above (below) non-profit sharers	7.4	7.8	0.4	3.4	0.8	6.6	14.5	11.0	6.5

% Return on sales

	1977/ 78	1978/ 79	1979/ 80	1980/ 81	1981/ 82	1982/ 83	1983/ 84	1984/ 85	Average 8 years
Profit sharing companies	15.3	15.9	12.3	8.6	9.2	9.3	11.4	7.8	11.2
Non-profit sharing companies	8.0	8.2	6.7	4.5	5.8	5.9	6.5	6.6	6.5
Difference: profit sharers above (below) non-profit sharers	7.3	7.7	5.6	4.1	3.4	3.4	4.9	1.2	4.7

% Growth in sales

	1977/ 78	1978/ 79	1979/ 80	1980/ 81	1981/ 82	1982/ 83	1983/ 84	1984/ 85	Average 8 years
Profit sharing companies	15.4	14.8	1.8	10.0	12.6	11.9	26.3	5.4	**12.3**
Non-profit sharing companies	12.1	10.4	16.8	(0.5)	4.8	14.1	8.3	18.9	**10.6**
Difference: profit sharers above (below) non-profit sharers	3.3	4.4	(15.0)	10.5	7.8	(2.2)	18.0	(13.5)	**1.7**

Dividends per share (pence)

	1977/ 78	1978/ 79	1979/ 80	1980/ 81	1981/ 82	1982/ 83	1983/ 84	1984/ 85	Average 8 years
Profit sharing companies	5.0	6.5	5.8	5.9	6.2	7.2	8.8	9.4	**6.9**
Non-profit sharing companies	3.7	5.1	5.2	5.4	5.8	6.2	6.9	7.0	**5.7**
Difference: profit sharers above (below) non-profit sharers	1.3	1.4	0.6	0.5	0.4	1.0	1.9	2.4	**1.2**

Total annual investor returns (%)

	1978	1979	1980	1981	1982	1983	1984	1985	Average 8 years
Profit sharing companies	50.4	15.9	0.9	10.3	46.4	14.0	26.2	17.9	**22.8**
Non-profit sharing companies	12.6	(1.2)	(6.5)	26.2	5.1	31.6	22.0	32.7	**15.3**
Difference: profit sharers above (below) non-profit sharers	37.8	17.1	7.4	(15.9)	41.3	(17.6)	4.2	(14.8)	**7.5**

Sector 3. Drapery and stores

Number of companies:

Profit sharing	19
Non-profit sharing	25
Total	44

Drapery and stores is one of the most homogeneous sectors, and the one in which, in our project, we have the nearest to equality in numbers of profit sharers and non-profit sharers. It therefore comes closest to providing an exact comparison on an individual sector basis of like with like.

% Return on capital employed

	1977/ 78	1978/ 79	1979/ 80	1980/ 81	1981/ 82	1982/ 83	1983/ 84	1984/ 85	Average 8 years
Profit sharing companies	26.2	30.3	21.4	16.2	14.8	17.0	20.1	17.8	20.5
Non-profit sharing companies	22.4	22.9	14.8	9.2	8.0	9.8	9.9	10.4	13.4
Difference: profit sharers above (below) non-profit sharers	3.8	7.4	6.6	7.0	6.8	7.2	10.2	7.4	7.1

Earnings per share (pence)

	1977/ 78	1978/ 79	1979/ 80	1980/ 81	1981/ 82	1982/ 83	1983/ 84	1984/ 85	Average 8 years
Profit sharing companies	11.8	16.4	12.6	13.1	10.2	10.0	16.3	15.9	13.3
Non-profit sharing companies	9.9	12.6	10.3	7.0	5.3	7.6	8.6	6.7	8.5
Difference: profit sharers above (below) non-profit sharers	1.9	3.8	2.3	6.1	4.9	2.4	7.7	9.2	4.8

% Return on sales

	1977/ 78	1978/ 79	1979/ 80	1980/ 81	1981/ 82	1982/ 83	1983/ 84	1984/ 85	Average 8 years
Profit sharing companies	7.7	8.6	6.6	5.2	5.1	6.0	7.2	7.2	6.7
Non-profit sharing companies	7.7	8.0	5.3	3.0	2.8	3.4	3.1	2.5	4.5
Difference: profit sharers above (below) non-profit sharers	0	0.6	1.3	2.2	2.3	2.6	4.1	4.7	2.2

% Growth in sales

	1977/ 78	1978/ 79	1979/ 80	1980/ 81	1981/ 82	1982/ 83	1983/ 84	1984/ 85	Average 8 years
Profit sharing companies	17.4	20.4	17.3	10.5	9.9	12.9	15.5	11.0	**14.4**
Non-profit sharing companies	16.5	16.8	9.8	3.3	2.7	3.6	9.2	12.9	**9.4**
Difference: profit sharers above (below) non-profit sharers	0.9	3.6	7.5	7.2	7.2	9.3	6.3	(1.9)	**5.0**

Dividends per share (pence)

	1977/ 78	1978/ 79	1979/ 80	1980/ 81	1981/ 82	1982/ 83	1983/ 84	1984/ 85	**Average 8 years**
Profit sharing companies	2.4	3.4	4.1	4.2	3.8	4.1	5.1	5.1	**4.0**
Non-profit sharing companies	3.1	3.6	3.8	2.9	2.9	2.8	3.3	3.2	**3.2**
Difference: profit sharers above (below) non-profit sharers	(0.7)	(0.2)	0.3	1.3	0.9	1.3	1.8	1.9	**0.8**

Total annual investor returns (%)

	1978	1979	1980	1981	1982	1983	1984	1985	Average 8 years
Profit sharing companies	29.5	16.3	5.8	10.1	61.3	21.9	49.1	46.0	**30.0**
Non-profit sharing companies	37.5	(6.3)	1.2	19.8	21.5	27.8	46.2	44.0	**24.0**
Difference: profit sharers above (below) non-profit sharers	(8.0)	22.6	4.6	(9.7)	39.8	(5.9)	2.9	2.0	**6.0**

Sector 4. Electricals

Number of companies:

Profit sharing	6
Non-profit sharing	23
Total	29

% Return on capital employed

	1977/ 78	1978/ 79	1979/ 80	1980/ 81	1981/ 82	1982/ 83	1983/ 84	1984/ 85	Average 8 years
Profit sharing companies	33.2	28.0	21.4	22.3	22.4	25.9	34.3	32.7	27.5
Non-profit sharing companies	28.7	25.9	25.8	22.1	24.0	26.3	28.6	22.7	25.5
Difference: profit sharers above (below) non-profit sharers	4.5	2.1	(4.4)	0.2	(1.6)	(0.4)	5.7	10.0	2.0

Earnings per share (pence)

	1977/ 78	1978/ 79	1979/ 80	1980/ 81	1981/ 82	1982/ 83	1983/ 84	1984/ 85	Average 8 years
Profit sharing companies	13.2	13.9	10.4	8.5	6.2	8.9	13.0	14.0	11.0
Non-profit sharing companies	13.5	15.8	16.7	8.6	14.2	14.6	13.9	15.1	14.0
Difference: profit sharers above (below) non-profit sharers	(0.3)	(1.9)	(6.3)	(0.1)	(8.0)	(5.7)	(0.9)	(1.1)	(3.0)

% Return on sales

	1977/ 78	1978/ 79	1979/ 80	1980/ 81	1981/ 82	1982/ 83	1983/ 84	1984/ 85	Average 8 years
Profit sharing companies	15.7	14.6	12.6	12.9	11.9	13.0	14.0	14.1	13.6
Non-profit sharing companies	11.7	10.9	10.2	8.4	10.8	13.0	12.7	11.4	11.1
Difference: profit sharers above (below) non-profit sharers	4.0	3.7	2.4	4.5	1.1	0	1.3	2.7	2.5

% Growth in sales

	1977/ 78	1978/ 79	1979/ 80	1980/ 81	1981/ 82	1982/ 83	1983/ 84	1984/ 85	Average 8 years
Profit sharing companies	22.0	19.9	22.9	8.7	10.2	15.9	20.5	16.7	**17.1**
Non-profit sharing companies	23.7	18.4	14.6	17.7	27.4	18.7	33.9	16.4	**21.4**
Difference: profit sharers above (below) non-profit sharers	(1.7)	1.5	8.3	(9.0)	(17.2)	(2.8)	(13.4)	0.3	**(4.3)**

Dividends per share (pence)

	1977/ 78	1978/ 79	1979/ 80	1980/ 81	1981/ 82	1982/ 83	1983/ 84	1984/ 85	Average 8 years
Profit sharing companies	3.7	4.5	4.5	3.7	3.1	3.4	4.0	4.4	**3.9**
Non-profit sharing companies	3.7	4.7	5.4	4.1	4.3	4.7	4.9	5.5	**4.7**
Difference: profit sharers above (below) non-profit sharers	0	(0.2)	(0.9)	(0.4)	(1.2)	(1.3)	(0.9)	(1.1)	**(0.8)**

Total annual investor returns (%)

	1978	1979	1980	1981	1982	1983	1984	1985	Average 8 years
Profit sharing companies	33.9	18.4	4.0	35.6	6.9	24.9	35.1	0.4	**19.9**
Non-profit sharing companies	27.3	2.7	30.1	28.2	33.2	7.8	14.5	(8.4)	**16.9**
Difference: profit sharers above (below) non-profit sharers	6.6	15.7	(26.1)	7.4	(26.3)	17.1	20.6	8.8	**3.0**

Sector 5. Engineering

Number of companies:

Profit sharing	10
Non-profit sharing	59
Total	69

% Return on capital employed

	1977/ 78	1978/ 79	1979/ 80	1980/ 81	1981/ 82	1982/ 83	1983/ 84	1984/ 85	Average 8 years
Profit sharing companies	23.2	20.9	14.1	6.4	8.0	8.0	12.7	16.6	13.7
Non-profit sharing companies	21.7	18.5	14.1	5.9	6.4	6.3	13.0	13.9	12.5
Difference: profit sharers above (below) non-profit sharers	1.5	2.4	0	0.5	1.6	1.7	(0.3)	2.7	1.2

Earnings per share (pence)

	1977/ 78	1978/ 79	1979/ 80	1980/ 81	1981/ 82	1982/ 83	1983/ 84	1984/ 85	Average 8 years
Profit sharing companies	15.3	17.1	14.2	7.8	8.8	7.4	12.4	14.2	12.2
Non-profit sharing companies	16.3	17.4	13.9	8.0	8.6	8.2	11.5	14.4	12.3
Difference: profit sharers above (below) non-profit sharers	(1.0)	(0.3)	0.3	(0.2)	0.2	(0.8)	0.9	(0.2)	(0.1)

% Return on sales

	1977/ 78	1978/ 79	1979/ 80	1980/ 81	1981/ 82	1982/ 83	1983/ 84	1984/ 85	Average 8 years
Profit sharing companies	9.4	8.5	6.3	1.9	3.4	4.8	6.1	7.9	6.0
Non-profit sharing companies	7.7	6.7	4.4	1.8	2.3	2.7	4.4	4.9	4.4
Difference: profit sharers above (below) non-profit sharers	1.7	1.8	1.9	0.1	1.1	2.1	1.7	3.0	1.6

% Growth in sales

	1977/ 78	1978/ 79	1979/ 80	1980/ 81	1981/ 82	1982/ 83	1983/ 84	1984/ 85	Average 8 years
Profit sharing companies	20.9	15.3	3.6	(10.4)	0.7	(0.2)	12.2	50.3	**11.5**
Non-profit sharing companies	17.2	17.1	15.0	(2.3)	8.2	(0.3)	10.9	10.3	**9.5**
Difference: profit sharers above (below) non-profit sharers	3.7	(1.8)	(11.4)	(8.1)	(7.5)	(0.1)	1.3	40.0	**2.0**

Dividends per share (pence)

	1977/ 78	1978/ 79	1979/ 80	1980/ 81	1981/ 82	1982/ 83	1983/ 84	1984/ 85	Average 8 years
Profit sharing companies	3.9	4.7	4.9	3.8	4.2	4.3	4.7	5.3	**4.5**
Non-profit sharing companies	4.4	5.3	5.2	4.4	4.6	4.6	5.2	5.3	**4.9**
Difference: profit sharers above (below) non-profit sharers	(0.5)	(0.6)	(0.3)	(0.6)	(0.4)	(0.3)	(0.5)	0	**(0.4)**

Total annual investor returns (%)

	1978	1979	1980	1981	1982	1983	1984	1985	Average 8 years
Profit sharing companies	33.3	(8.3)	(6.0)	19.4	(8.0)	24.2	52.6	21.8	**16.1**
Non-profit sharing companies	21.5	(9.4)	(6.4)	9.3	(5.9)	24.9	34.2	36.7	**13.1**
Difference: profit sharers above (below) non-profit sharers	11.8	1.1	0.4	10.1	(2.1)	(0.7)	18.4	(14.9)	**3.0**

Sector 6. Food, groceries etc.

Number of companies:

Profit sharing	8
Non-profit sharing	21
Total	29

% Return on capital employed

	1977/ 78	1978/ 79	1979/ 80	1980/ 81	1981/ 82	1982/ 83	1983/ 84	1984/ 85	Average 8 years
Profit sharing companies	27.5	27.2	27.9	25.3	29.0	25.7	26.8	27.3	27.1
Non-profit sharing companies	21.6	23.9	21.7	22.2	18.6	19.6	16.9	14.1	19.8
Difference: profit sharers above (below) non-profit sharers	5.9	3.3	6.2	3.1	10.4	6.1	9.9	13.2	7.3

Earnings per share (pence)

	1977/ 78	1978/ 79	1979/ 80	1980/ 81	1981/ 82	1982/ 83	1983/ 84	1984/ 85	Average 8 years
Profit sharing companies	13.3	15.7	18.4	18.3	15.8	15.5	18.3	19.6	16.9
Non-profit sharing companies	10.2	14.3	16.0	13.6	14.9	17.2	17.2	16.7	15.0
Difference: profit sharers above (below) non-profit sharers	3.1	1.4	2.4	4.7	0.9	(1.7)	1.1	2.9	1.9

% Return on sales

	1977/ 78	1978/ 79	1979/ 80	1980/ 81	1981/ 82	1982/ 83	1983/ 84	1984/ 85	Average 8 years
Profit sharing companies	5.2	5.2	5.1	5.0	4.5	4.6	4.7	5.3	5.0
Non-profit sharing companies	3.2	4.0	3.5	3.9	3.5	3.9	3.7	2.8	3.6
Difference: profit sharers above (below) non-profit sharers	2.0	1.2	1.6	1.1	1.0	0.7	1.0	2.5	1.4

% Growth in sales

	1977/ 78	1978/ 79	1979/ 80	1980/ 81	1981/ 82	1982/ 83	1983/ 84	1984/ 85	Average 8 years
Profit sharing companies	21.9	19.2	25.0	17.6	41.5	12.2	14.2	7.7	19.9
Non-profit sharing companies	15.0	15.1	17.2	12.5	12.6	15.8	11.4	5.1	13.1
Difference: profit sharers above (below) non-profit sharers	6.9	4.1	7.8	5.1	28.9	(3.6)	2.8	2.6	6.8

Dividends per share (pence)

	1977/ 78	1978/ 79	1979/ 80	1980/ 81	1981/ 82	1982/ 83	1983/ 84	1984/ 85	Average 8 years
Profit sharing companies	2.7	3.7	4.5	5.0	5.0	5.4	6.5	6.4	4.9
Non-profit sharing companies	3.4	3.9	4.9	4.6	4.9	5.6	6.1	6.7	5.0
Difference: profit sharers above (below) non-profit sharers	(0.7)	(0.2)	(0.4)	0.4	0.1	(0.2)	0.4	(0.3)	(0.1)

Total annual investor returns (%)

	1978	1979	1980	1981	1982	1983	1984	1985	Average 8 years
Profit sharing companies	23.8	21.9	73.7	25.1	32.4	14.8	20.2	28.4	30.0
Non-profit sharing companies	20.0	19.4	15.7	20.4	30.4	24.2	28.9	22.5	22.7
Difference: profit sharers above (below) non-profit sharers	3.8	2.5	58.0	4.7	2.0	(9.4)	(8.7)	5.9	7.3

Sector 7. Miscellaneous

Number of companies:
Profit sharing   54
Non-profit sharing   121
Total   175

With the larger number of companies in this sector (which includes beers, wines and spirits; industrials – miscellaneous; paper, printing, advertising; and textiles) the results largely reflect those of the composite results in Chapter 5.

% Return on capital employed

	1977/ 78	1978/ 79	1979/ 80	1980/ 81	1981/ 82	1982/ 83	1983/ 84	1984/ 85	Average 8 years
Profit sharing companies	28.1	25.4	18.3	15.2	15.9	19.2	20.8	20.7	20.4
Non-profit sharing companies	23.1	20.8	14.0	8.6	8.9	11.0	16.0	17.0	14.9
Difference: profit sharers above (below) non-profit sharers	5.0	4.6	4.3	6.6	7.0	8.2	4.8	3.7	5.5

Earnings per share (pence)

	1977/ 78	1978/ 79	1979/ 80	1980/ 81	1981/ 82	1982/ 83	1983/ 84	1984/ 85	Average 8 years
Profit sharing companies	14.8	17.2	15.5	14.3	14.9	16.8	20.4	19.5	16.7
Non-profit sharing companies	14.3	16.5	12.8	8.5	7.5	10.7	17.0	17.2	13.1
Difference: profit sharers above (below) non-profit sharers	0.5	0.7	2.7	5.8	7.4	6.1	3.4	2.3	3.6

% Return on sales

	1977/ 78	1978/ 79	1979/ 80	1980/ 81	1981/ 82	1982/ 83	1983/ 84	1984/ 85	Average 8 years
Profit sharing companies	11.6	10.7	9.3	7.3	7.7	8.6	8.9	8.8	9.1
Non-profit sharing companies	8.3	8.1	5.1	3.9	3.6	4.8	6.4	6.4	5.8
Difference: profit sharers above (below) non-profit sharers	3.3	2.6	4.2	3.4	4.1	3.8	2.5	2.4	3.3

% Growth in sales

	1977/ 78	1978/ 79	1979/ 80	1980/ 81	1981/ 82	1982/ 83	1983/ 84	1984/ 85	Average 8 years
Profit sharing companies	23.5	18.7	13.8	15.6	11.2	11.8	19.3	15.2	**16.1**
Non-profit sharing companies	18.1	20.3	14.4	13.4	8.2	14.2	15.0	13.8	**14.7**
Difference: profit sharers above (below) non-profit sharers	5.4	(1.6)	(0.6)	2.2	3.0	(2.4)	4.3	1.4	**1.4**

Dividends per share (pence)

	1977/ 78	1978/ 79	1979/ 80	1980/ 81	1981/ 82	1982/ 83	1983/ 84	1984/ 85	Average 8 years
Profit sharing companies	3.8	4.8	5.0	4.8	5.2	6.0	6.8	7.4	**5.5**
Non-profit sharing companies	4.2	5.1	5.0	5.1	5.0	5.2	5.8	6.3	**5.2**
Difference: profit sharers above (below) non-profit sharers	(0.4)	(0.3)	0	(0.3)	0.2	0.8	1.0	1.1	**0.3**

Total annual investor returns (%)

	1978	1979	1980	1981	1982	1983	1984	1985	Average 8 years
Profit sharing companies	30.2	7.1	14.0	19.5	44.7	22.3	31.0	27.0	**24.5**
Non-profit sharing companies	28.0	0.2	6.7	11.9	12.4	36.5	27.7	24.2	**18.5**
Difference: profit sharers above (below) non-profit sharers	2.2	6.9	7.3	7.6	32.3	(14.2)	3.3	2.8	**6.0**

Profit sharing companies included in the project, listed by sector

Sector 1: Building, timber, roads	Year profit sharing started
Barratt Developments PLC	1980
Blue Circle Industries PLC	1975
Costain Group PLC	1979
Countryside Properties PLC	1979
The Henderson Group PLC	1980
Walter Lawrence PLC	1980
A. Monk & Company PLC	1981
The Rugby Portland Cement PLC	1939
Rush & Tompkins Group PLC	1979
Watts, Blake, Bearne and Company PLC	1979

Sector 2: Chemicals, plastics	
Horace Cory PLC	1980
James Halstead Group PLC	1980
Imperial Chemical Industries PLC	1954
William Ransom & Son PLC	1981
Rentokil Group PLC	1960
Wolstenholme Rink PLC	1981

Sector 3: Drapery and stores	
James Beattie PLC	1947

Bentalls PLC	1974
British Home Stores PLC	1977
The Burton Group PLC	1979
Church & Co. PLC	1980
Courts (Furnishers) PLC	1980
Debenhams PLC	1981
Foster Brothers Clothing PLC	1979
J. Hepworth & Son PLC	1980
Home Charm PLC	1980
House of Fraser PLC	1978
Liberty PLC	1981
MFI Furniture Group PLC	1981
Marks and Spencer PLC	1978
John Menzies PLC	1981
Owen Owen PLC	1974
Alfred Preedy & Sons PLC	1924
Austin Reed Group PLC	1981
W.H. Smith & Son (Holdings) PLC	1981

Sector 4: Electricals

Electronic Rentals Group PLC	1979
Farnell Electronics PLC	1981
Rotaflex PLC	1981
Telephone Rentals PLC	1946
F.W. Thorpe PLC	1960
Unitech PLC	1970

Sector 5: Engineering

The Birmingham Mint PLC	1980
Burgess Products (Holdings) PLC	1981
Desoutter Brothers (Holdings) PLC	1979
Downiebrae Holdings PLC	1974
Edbro (Holdings) PLC	1960
IMI PLC	1962
Meggitt Holdings PLC	1980
Molins PLC	1977
Ratcliffs (Great Bridge) PLC	1969
Rotork PLC	1979

Sector 6: Food, groceries, etc.

Avana Group PLC	1980
Bejam Group PLC	1981
Maynards PLC	1980
Wm. Morrison Supermarkets PLC	1979
Northern Foods PLC	1980
Nurdin & Peacock PLC	1980
Rowntree Mackintosh PLC	1981
J. Sainsbury PLC	1980

Sector 7: Miscellaneous

Bass PLC	1980
Beecham Group PLC	1955
Belhaven Brewery Group PLC	1978
Arthur Bell & Sons PLC	1980
The Boots Company PLC	1955
Brook Street Bureau PLC	1979
Matthew Brown PLC	1978
Buckley's Brewery PLC	1981
H.P. Bulmer Holdings PLC	1979
Chamberlain Phipps PLC	1980
Charter Consolidated PLC	1981
Christies International PLC	1979
Richard Clay PLC	1943
Corah PLC	1981
Cosalt PLC	1980
Courtney Pope (Holdings) PLC	1959
James Cropper PLC	1950
Dawson International PLC	1975
J.A. Devenish PLC	1979
Dinkie Heel PLC	1979
English China Clays PLC	1964
Feedex Agricultural Industries PLC	1980
Ferguson Industrial Holdings PLC	1971
Fisons PLC	1970
Forshaws Burtonwood Brewery PLC	1979
Fothergill & Harvey PLC	1980
Fuller, Smith & Turner PLC	1981
Glaxo Holdings PLC	1955

Granada Group PLC	1980
Greene, King & Sons PLC	1980
Arthur Guinness & Sons PLC	1964
Halma PLC	1980
Philip Harris (Holdings) PLC	1978
Hoskins & Horton PLC	1979
Irish Distillers Group PLC	1974
Johnson Group Cleaners PLC	1980
Kalamazoo PLC	1948
Macarthys Pharmaceuticals PLC	1961
Marston, Thompson and Evershed PLC	1981
More O'Ferrall PLC	1979
Nu-Swift Industries PLC	1952
R.F.D. Group PLC	1981
Reckitt & Colman PLC	1961
Reed Executive PLC	1980
Alexander Russell PLC	1979
Sale Tilney PLC	1981
Sketchley PLC	1979
Trafalgar House PLC	1979
Vaux Breweries PLC	1979
Wedgwood PLC	1975
Whatman Reeve Angel PLC	1979
Whitbread and Company PLC	1979
Wolseley-Hughes PLC	1975
Young and Co.'s Brewery PLC	1964

Bibliography

1. Official Reports

Schloss, D.F. *Report on Profit Sharing*, HMSO 1894, Cmnd. 7458

Barnes, G.S. *Report on Profit Sharing and Labour Co-Partnership in the United Kingdom*, HMSO 1912, Cmnd. 6496

Hilton, J. *Report on Profit Sharing and Labour Co-Partnership in the United Kingdom*, HMSO 1920, Cmnd. 544

'Profit Sharing and Co-Partnership in 1938' *Ministry of Labour Gazette*, (August 1939) pp. 288–290

'Profit Sharing and Co-Partnership Schemes' *Ministry of Labour Gazette*, (May 1956) pp. 165–169

2. Books and other Reports and Articles

Adams, R. *Participation Today*, Industrial Participation Association (1984)

Bell, D. Wallace. *Financial Participation*, Industrial Participation Association (1973)

Bell, D. Wallace. *Industrial Participation*, Pitman (1979)

Bell, D. Wallace. *Profit Sharing and Employee Shareholding Report*, Industrial Participation Association (1980)

Bell, D. Wallace and Hanson, C. G. *Profit Sharing and Employee Shareholding Attitude Survey*, Industrial Participation Association (1984) Note: The survey is available only from the IPA's office at 85, Tooley Street, London SE1 2QZ. (01-403 6018), price £19–50 including postage and packing

Britain's Industrial Future (The Yellow Book), Report of the Liberal Industrial Inquiry of 1928, Ernest Benn (1928) reprinted 1977

Hanson, C. G. 'Profit Sharing Schemes in Great Britain', *Management Studies*, (Oct. 1965) pp. 331–350

Latta, G. W. *Profit Sharing, Employee Stock Ownership, Savings, and Asset Formation Plans in the Western World*, University of Pennsylvania (The Wharton School) (1979)

Metzger, Bert L. (Ed.) *Profit Sharing*, Profit Sharing Research Foundation (USA) (1982)

Mond, Sir Alfred *Industry and Politics*, Macmillan (1927)

Smith, G.R. 'Profit sharing and employee share ownership in Britain', *Employment Gazette*, (Sept. 1986) pp. 380–385

Steel, David, M.P., *Sharing Profits*, Unservile State Papers Number 33, Hebden Royd Publications Ltd (1986)

Wallace, William. *Prescription for Partnership*, Pitman (1959)

INDEX

The Index does not include references to profit and profit sharing which are the theme of the whole book, nor to the economic ratios used in the comparison of the economic performance of profit sharing and non-profit sharing companies. Nor does it duplicate the list of profit sharing companies in Appendix 2.